DONALD EDGAR
THE ROYAL PARKS

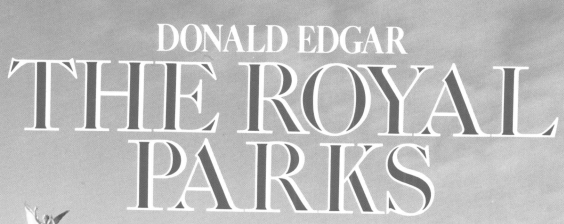

W.H. ALLEN · LONDON
1986

Set in Plantin by Phoenix Photosetting, Chatham, Kent
Printed and bound in Singapore
for the Publishers, W.H. Allen & Co. Plc
44 Hill Street, London W1X 8LB

British Library Cataloguing in Publication Data

Edgar, Donald
    The royal parks.
    1. Parks—England—London—History
    I. Title
    942.1   DA689.P2

ISBN 0 491 03592 6

'What had been the delights of the lord
are now the delights of the people.'

(Deliciae populi, quae fuerant domini.)

Martial, *De Spectaculis* II 12, of land
given to public use

At Hampton Court there are 27 'grace and favour' residences in the palace which are solely at the Queen's disposal. Altogether there are 121 such residences, including 13 at Kensington Palace and 20 at St James's, including York House.

At Greenwich two fine palaces designed by two of our most outstanding architects, Inigo Jones and Christopher Wren, now house important national institutions – the Royal Naval College and the National Maritime Museum.

In Kew Gardens the royal associations are everywhere, from the little Dutch 'Palace' to the 'Queen's Cottage' hidden in the dark, very Germanic, pinetarium.

Kew was the family home for forty years of George III, his Queen, Charlotte, and their fifteen children and it holds many happy as well as sad memories.

Windsor Castle is for the Queen 'my home'. The vast pile dominates the Home Park, the Great Park and the surrounding countryside: for it is the largest of the royal palaces with an estimated 680 rooms. Buckingham Palace has rather more than 600; Sandringham (after recent demolitions) about 550 and Balmoral around 250.

The Queen is often at Windsor. When she is at Buckingham Palace she likes to spend the weekend there. She likes to gather the whole family there for Christmas. At Easter she tries to spend about four weeks at the castle and in June goes back for a week to attend the Royal Ascot race meeting nearby. Whilst the Queen is in residence at Windsor various official and ceremonial occasions take place, of which the most splendid is the annual procession of the Knights of the Garter which she leads into St George's Chapel.

So it is that although the upkeep of these Royal Parks has been for long defrayed by the taxes of the public which in return has the right of access, the ambience of royalty, both past and present, remains.

The Parks wear a domesticated air with their planned avenues and copses of trees, their carefully tended beds of flowers, their artificial lakes and all the necessary (and welcome) adjuncts of sign-posts, litter-bins, lavatories, cafeteria and restaurants.

The herds of deer at Greenwich and Windsor, even among the bracken of Richmond Park, are gracefully decorative. It was not always so. When William of Normandy conquered England he treated the Kingdom as his own. The royal estate was a third of all the land and the royal forests a sixth. The herds of deer and other game were protected by savage laws.

At that time in the 11th century England was a primitive land of forest and marsh with agriculture confined to clearings round towns, villages and monastic foundations, linked by worn paths. The elaborate, civilised infrastructure of the flourishing Roman colony, Britannia, with its network of roads linking

11

planned towns in a landscape of fertile fields, orchards and vineyards interspersed with sumptuous villas had been utterly destroyed by successive waves of northern barbarians from whom many of us are descended.

For the Norman and Angevin Kings of England the forests were farmed for meat, especially venison, to feed the royal family, the court officials, guards and trains of hangers-on. Food was not plentiful. Bread, meat and ale were the staple diet.

When meat was needed from the royal forests the deer were driven by beaters, rather as in a grouse or partridge shoot today, towards a line of hunters, concealed at the edge of a wood. They had to be placed near the run of the deer for the effective range of an arrow from a longbow was no more than fifty yards.

This was deer-farming, but there was another much more exciting and prestigious way of pursuing game – the hunt.

The Royal Parks of today are, for the most part, relics of royal hunting preserves. The purpose of the hunt was not, except fortuitously, the pursuit of game for food; it was to satisfy the primeval desire to kill, with all the embellishments of elaborate ceremonial dress and customs, the coded notes of the horns, the baying ('music') of hounds and the ritual disembowelling of the prey.

If the original purpose of Royal Parks was to enclose and preserve game, especially the herds of deer, another gentler use of the ground was modestly practised in medieval times within the shelter of castle walls and moats: the cultivation of gardens.

The times were violent and everywhere men built walls to protect cities, towns, ports, river crossings and any vulnerable point. The king and his feudal nobles lived almost imprisoned in their own castles. The gardens which surrounded them were, like those of the monastic foundations, primarily for practical use rather than pleasure. Herbs were grown for medicines and flavouring; an orchard was cultivated for fruit and a flower garden for blooms to deck the table and adorn the altar, and to perfume the ladies' chambers.

These castle gardens were high-walled, perhaps not only for security but because it was an inward-looking age, and as Derek Clifford says in his masterly *History of Garden Design*, 'men were too preoccupied with the survival of their bodies in this world and of their souls in the next to refine very much upon the art of living'.

Yet, before the Italian Renaissance made the world young again and the Medici and their brilliant circle renewed the ideals of the classical gardens outside Florence, it was not entirely a dark, colourless picture north of the Alps. As Dillian Gordon writes in her excellent commentaries on *100 Great Paintings in the National Gallery*, very little English medieval art has survived, but there are illustrations of gardens in Europe

12

and although they probably portray a higher civilisation than obtained in England at the time, nevertheless the court of, say, Richard II, who reigned from 1381 to 1399, reflected some of the sophisticated elegance of the life that he had known as a boy in Bordeaux, then part of the Angevin Empire.

There is a garden scene* memorable for its poignancy in Shakespeare's *Richard II* when the French Queen, Catherine, is trying to assuage her mounting fears for her husband in the peace of the garden of the Duke of York at Langley.

Shakespeare was writing in the second half of the 16th century, but his genius, as so often, overcomes time. We are in the garden in 1399 when the Queen and her two ladies conceal themselves as the gardener appears with two assistants. One of them soon finds an excuse not to work:

'Why should we . . . .
When our sea-walled garden, the whole land,
Is full of weeds, her fairest flowers choked up,
Her fruit-trees all unpruned, her hedges ruin'd,
Her knots disorder'd, and her wholesome herbs
Swarming with caterpillars?'

Those lines encompass much of the medieval garden and introduce the 'knots' or patterns of earth or box which were with increasing intricacy dividing up the flower-beds. Writing about the same time as Shakespeare, Francis Bacon, in his memorable essay 'Of Gardens' was highly critical of them:

'As for the making of Knots or figures with divers-coloured earths, that they may lie under the windows of the house on that side which the garden stands, they be but toys: you may see as good sights many times in tarts.'

Shakespeare and Bacon, splendid jewels of the English genius, were children of the miraculous Renaissance. Francis I, 'Prince of the Renaissance', although in many ways a disastrous failure, permanently enriched the cultural life of France. The palace and gardens of Fontainebleau, which were created at his behest out of a wilderness, were not only an enchanting world of his own ('chez moi'), but soon became a wonder of the Western world. Henry VIII of England, always trying in parvenu fashion to rival his more powerful and rich contemporary monarchs, Francis and the Emperor Charles V, decided after hearing about Fontainebleau to build a bigger and better palace and gardens at Nonsuch, near Epsom in Surrey.

The grounds of Fontainebleau were described as containing 'many lovely gardens and groves and beautiful fountains'. The main feature was a large decorative lake which could be considered a forerunner of the Serpentine in Hyde Park or the lake in front of Blenheim Palace.

Following pages: Deer in Richmond Park.

* Act III, Scene IV.

13

Many developments of garden design in Italy, France and the Low Countries were to influence the royal Parks. But English parks and gardens were also to develop their own genius. Grass lawns, which probably owed their origin to bowling greens, flourished as nowhere else thanks to climate, soil and careful choice of seed. In the 18th century inspired changes were brought about by the English creation of landscape gardening, furthered by the great gifts of Lancelot 'Capability' Brown.

As the world was opened by conquest, trade and exploration, trees and plants were brought to England in increasing profusion. The Chelsea Physick Garden early played an important part in the nurturing of exotic species, but the great impetus was given by the botanical garden created in the grounds of their home at Kew by Prince Frederick, heir to George II, and his wife, Princess Augusta of Saxe Gotha. Prince Frederick died as Prince of Wales, and Augusta carried on the gardens at Kew with the assistance of Lord Bute, an expert botanist, who was widely believed to solace her widowhood. He later became the Prime Minister of Augusta's son, George III, and helped to lose the American colonies.

At the end of the Napoleonic Wars Britain's navies controlled the oceans of the world, linking her overseas possessions and furthering her trade. Royal Navy ships were used to carry botanists and bring back even more exotic trees and plants. Britain had for a time almost a monopoly in these goods.

After the death of George III the botanical gardens at Kew were neglected, but in 1838 a Committee of Parliament recommended their work was so valuable that they should be taken over by the State. Thus began the establishment of the Royal Botanic Gardens and their rise to world fame, supervised by scientists of outstanding ability. Their botanists, often at great personal risk, scoured the world and found fantastic orchids in steamy tropical forests, magnolias and camellias on the hillsides of Sin-kiang in China and rhododendrons in the Himalayas, covering the misty mountainsides with banks of colour. It was an exciting time and that excitement can still be felt at Kew — perhaps in one of the splendid glasshouses that were built in the great Victorian age of creativity.

It is our good fortune that the Royal Parks are available to us as a living heritage. In them are to be seen all the history of their past, from herds of deer in woods and bracken and walled medieval gardens to stretches of open landscape and carefully grouped displays of flowering plants.

16

Hyde Park and Kensington Gardens:

The King's Takeover

ALTHOUGH THESE TWO great Royal Parks in Central London bear different names and have developed such different personalities, they form a continuous stretch of 600 acres which until 1536 was a farm belonging to Westminster Abbey.

In that year Henry VIII decided he wanted a more spacious hunting park than St James's provided and arbitrarily took over this abbey land that lay nearby, giving in exchange a priory and estate in Berkshire. It is significant that in this same year, 1536, Henry had ordered Anne Boleyn, his second wife, to be beheaded for alleged infidelity. For a man of overweening pride such as Henry, St James's Palace and the surrounding Park must have been from then on a source of tortured memories, for he had created the setting as much for Anne as for himself in his years of infatuation.

The new royal Hyde Park was enclosed with palings and well stocked with herds of deer. The fields were no longer tilled and soon reverted to scrubland with the Westbourne stream and attendant marshy pools the haunt of wildfowl. Hares, pheasants and partridges also abounded. The northern and eastern boundaries (now the Bayswater Road and Park Lane) lay roughly along two Roman roads – the Via Trinobantium which ran from Southampton to Colchester, and Watling Street on its way from Dover to Chester.

When Henry's daughter by Anne Boleyn, Queen Elizabeth, came to the throne, she put Hyde Park to good use. She invited visiting royalty, princes and ambassadors to splendid parties there, which were followed by banquets, music and dancing in the large lodge erected within the boundaries.

She also opened up the Park as a military training ground and rode out to inspect the troops and give them heart. Her encouragement was certainly needed at the time when England was gravely threatened by the Armada of Philip II of Spain (the widower of her half-sister, Mary, Queen of England, 1553–59).

Elizabeth was the last of the Tudor monarchs and was succeeded by James I, a descendant of her aunt, Margaret, who

17

had married the Stuart King James IV of Scotland. The new King shared with Elizabeth a background of family violence. Elizabeth's mother, Anne Boleyn, had been beheaded by her father, Henry VIII, and James's mother, Mary, Queen of Scots, had been beheaded by Elizabeth herself for treachery.

The new King adopted a liberal policy towards Hyde Park. The deer were penned into an enclosure except when a hunt was to take place, and at other times the public was given access.

Refreshment booths were soon set up in the Park, with such names as Cake House, Mince Pie House and Cheesecake House. On May Day, still an almost pagan festivity, there were maypoles, dancing and all the fun of the fair.

James's son, King Charles I, built a grand hunting lodge in the Park and entertained his guests in royal fashion. He had been seventeen years on the throne (1625–42), ruling with increasing despotism, before the patience of the English ran out.

The King raised his standard at Nottingham, but London, rich, resourceful and populous, was to be the unyielding centre of resistance and Hyde Park became an armed camp where the City's 'Trained Bands' exercised and kept watch over the western approaches. The days of ribboned maypoles, dancing, merrymaking and ribald songs had no place in these stern, puritanical years.

When Cromwell and Parliament ('The Rump' that was left of it) defeated the royal forces and the King was beheaded (1649), a Commission was set up to sell all the royal property, including the Parks, ostensibly to help with the national finances, but probably partly in a spirit of revenge.

The 600 acres of Hyde Park were sold off to three property speculators and the deer to landowners with private parks, and to butchers (1652). The proceeds were allocated to the Navy.

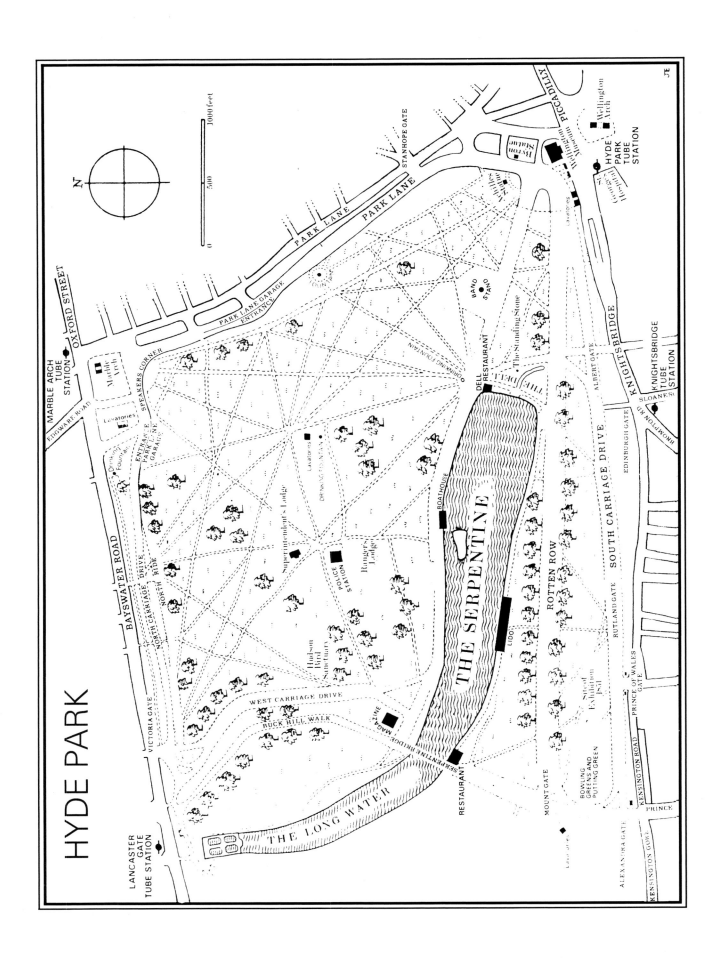

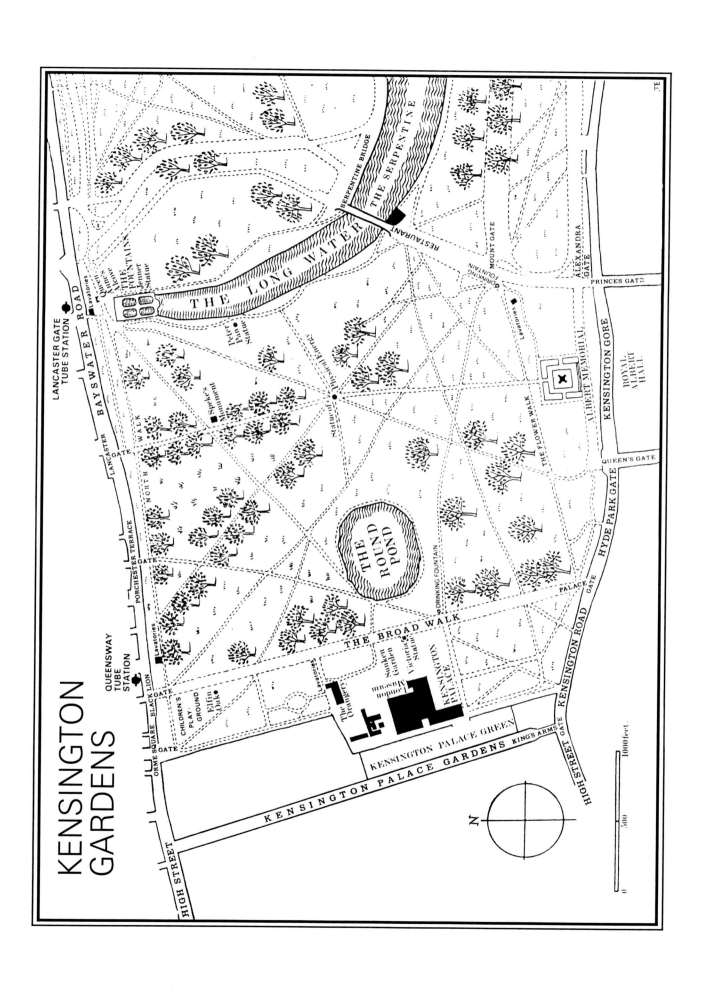

All seemed lost. The property speculators, however, were evidently prudent men, contenting themselves with charging exorbitant entrance fees for visitors, their coaches and horses. Their days of possession were not to last long, for in 1660 Charles II landed at Dover and was received with joy and acclamation in London.

The men who had bought Hyde Park were dispossessed, but the King in his clever, amiable way saw that they were recompensed. Soon the Park was basking in royal favour, and, it might be added, the favour of the royal favourites.

It was the Ring that made Hyde Park famous in that licentious Restoration society. To be anybody, to hope to be anybody, it was essential to be seen from time to time in the Ring. As with so many fashionable resorts in English social history, this entailed a considerable expense of time, money and self-respect.

The Ring had been laid out in the reign of Charles I roughly where the police station is now, a little to the north of the Serpentine. It consisted of two wide concentric tracks which seem to have been used at first for elegant displays of horsemanship and occasional foot-races run for a wager.

In the reign of Charles II, however, the Ring, with the traffic organised to flow in opposite directions along the two adjacent tracks, became the carriage drive for royalty, the nobility, the powerful, the rich, their women and those who aspired to this magic circle.

What a splendid sight it must have been on a sunny day! There were the men, vain as peacocks in full wigs under elaborate hats, embroidered coats, breeches, silk stockings and silver-buckled shoes.

As for the women – they were lush Restoration beauties, their hair in ringlets, their eyes skilfully enhanced by cosmetics, jewels sparkling on sumptuous creamy flesh, their swelling bosoms more or less covered by blue, gold or pink silk. Many of them looked as vapid as the cows which grazed in the Park. The look was often misleading as for the most part they had a shrewd eye for the main chance in life, whether as wife or mistress.

Both Evelyn, the diarist of the haut ton, and Pepys, the aspiring bourgeois, were often there and have left their accounts of the Ring. It is ironic that Pepys, who as we know was as lustful as the next man, made disparaging remarks about Barbara Palmer, later Duchess of Cleveland. Agreed, she was probably the most rapacious of the royal mistresses, but perhaps it was her insolence that made her unpopular – she would lie back half-asleep in her carriage in the Ring, superb in, say, yellow satin, quickly coming to life when the King appeared in the opposite direction. She would then engage him in intimate gossip for half an hour or more while the rest of the carriages waited, half-impatiently, half-enviously.

23

No one would have dared to complain at the delay. Probably no one would have wanted to complain at the delay! It was a splendid subject for 'one-upmanship' conversation for a few days.

For the King these affable drives in the Ring, like his promenades with his spaniels in St James's Park, were part of a brilliantly executed public relations programme to restore the popularity of the monarchy.

Undoubtedly, the excursions also owed much to his memories of the magnificent court of Louis XIV at Versailles which he knew from his years of exile. Louis had his promenades and carriage drives, though they were organised in an ambience of splendour and grandeur which Charles could never hope to rival. Nevertheless, it is likely that Charles remembered that Louis had a meticulously graduated greeting for those he passed on his walks, and that the carriage processions following a royal hunt were a triumph of precedence, taking account of his Queen, the royal family and the current order of favour of his mistresses.

Leaving aside, however, the vastly superior wealth and power of Louis XIV, it is difficult to believe that Charles II would ever have wanted so much formality in his court. Louis behaved with aloof dignity to all, Charles had a certain vulgar raffishness – which endeared him greatly to a nation tired of censorious Puritanism.

Charles put on a great show. He probably came to enjoy his own act!

In contrast to these scenes of fashion, beauty and gallantry, Hyde Park witnessed despair, destitution and death in the year of the Great Plague, 1665. In the City of London, Westminster and the surrounding parishes more than 100,000 men, women and children died from the contagion. This was out of a total population at the time estimated at no more than 450,000.

The court, the nobles, the rich and those with some small resources moved to the country. The poor, living in foul alleys or the insanitary rookeries outside the City's walls, were dying like the rats that had brought the Plague, and in desperation moved out of London in such numbers they could not be restrained. Some went to Epping and other nearby open spaces, but many moved to Hyde Park with their scant belongings and tools of their trades, setting up impromptu camps with the resource and ingenuity of the dispossessed.

Many still died of the foul disease and were buried unnamed in charnel pits, but the change of scene and the fresh air brought some solace and by autumn the Plague had abated. Gradually they broke up their camps and drifted back to their employments and their slums.

Death, however, was never far from the Park. Near Marble Arch is the site of the Tyburn gallows where over the centuries

Previous page: Hyde Park, seen from the top of the Hilton Hotel on Park Lane.

The Marble Arch was erected close to the site of the Tyburn gallows. Here seen as it looked at the time of the Great Exhibition of 1851, the Arch originally stood in front of the courtyard of Buckingham Palace facing down the Mall.

thousands of men met their end in public hangings which did not cease until 1818. The 'Tyburn Tree' developed in time into a 12 ft high triangular scaffold on which 24 men could be hanged at a time. Many of those who were sent on their final journeys all the way from the City of London and Westminster by cart or on foot were murderers, highwaymen and dangerous criminals. Others were convicted for offences which would today seem trivial, others again, mainly Catholic priests, were condemned for bravely refusing to abjure their faith. The bodies of the great Cromwell and his lieutenants, Ireton and Bradshaw, were exhumed and hanged there in a fit of hysterical revenge after the Restoration.

25

Hyde Park, then to Constitution Hill, past Green Park and on to St James's Palace and Horse Guards Parade. It was called the 'Route de Roi' which was gradually anglicised into 'Rotten Row'.* The new highway was lit by 300 tall oil-burning lamps during the dark months. This was quite an innovation for London and a wise move, for William's life was always to be in danger from assassins – Jacobites, Catholics, desperadoes in the pay of France and the riff-raff of the taverns of Covent Garden.

Henry Wise, a very able gardener, with his partner, George London, of Brompton Nurseries, the first large-scale business of its kind, were given the contract to lay out the gardens of Kensington House (it was not called a palace until later in the 18th century).

William liked designing gardens (he had laid out the grounds of Het Loo, his home in Holland), but the designs were, inevitably, the geometrical Dutch gardens of the 17th century. The central feature was a broad tree-lined avenue which ran down from the terrace in front of the King's Gallery. On either side were formal parterres planted with dwarf trees set in designs of box, sometimes circular, sometimes arabesque. There was said to be one parterre where the topiary work formed a fortification, 'The Siege of Troy'. It is worth mentioning that the formal Dutch gardens which had some influence here were not all that different from the classical French gardens created by Le Nôtre for Louis XIV. Perhaps it was more a European than a national style?

The Kensington gardens were quite extensive and were said to have covered 26 acres. Some acres of Hyde Park had been taken over – a forerunner of greater encroachments to come.

There was always work going on at Kensington House, now greatly extended, especially after the fire in 1691 when William and Mary narrowly escaped being burnt in their beds.

House and gardens continued to be improved. Orange, lemon and myrtle trees were set in tubs during the summer months to provide exotic colour (in winter they were preserved in Wise and London's greenhouses). For the Queen these were happy years, in spite of her husband's absences.

Then in 1694 at the age of 32 she caught smallpox. Fortunately, William was with her in Kensington. She sent away as many servants as possible when she learned of her infection. William was by nature a taciturn, hard man, who never spoke English fluently, probably deliberately. His attentions to Mary on her sick-bed and his tears and muttered prayers at her death do much to soften final opinions of this most remarkable Dutchman, King of England, Scotland and Ireland.

* Rotten Row was replaced in the 1730s by 'the King's New Road', now the South Carriage Drive. The section of Rotten Row in Hyde Park became (and has remained, more or less) a fashionable riding track.

31

In February 1696 the leaders of a band of forty or more conspirators began to plot the murder of the King which was to precede a Jacobite insurrection and the landing on the south-east coast of James II and a French army.

One of the plans considered by the conspirators was for resolute men to scale the walls of Kensington House at night, break into the building, overpower the guards (not more than twenty in number) and kill the King. This plan was, however, abandoned as were others, such as holding up the King's coach on a Sunday morning at Hyde Park Corner when he was on his way to church at St James's Chapel (where he had married Mary). The final decision was to kill the King when he was on his way to hunt in Richmond Park. He had to stop at Turnham Green to cross by the ferry and this was to be the assassins' moment.

As so often with Jacobite plots, the plans were betrayed. In Kensington House the King questioned 'the gentleman' who in return for immunity sent his friends to the gallows at Tyburn.

As a postscript, neither James nor the French army crossed the Channel.

By this time it was only William's indomitable will that kept him going, for his health was failing. In 1697, however, Louis XIV was forced to sign the Treaty of Ryswick, abandoning the Stuarts and recognising William as King. As Green writes in his *History of the English People*, it was 'the final and decisive defeat of the conspiracy to turn England into a Roman Catholic country and into a dependency of France'.

It is worth remembering those words on your next visit to the Gardens when you pass the statue of William III* in front of the King's Gallery.

In February 1702, William had a fall from his horse whilst riding at Hampton Court. It was too much for his enfeebled frame. He was brought back to Kensington to die in the house he and Mary had created.

William was succeeded by Anne, the younger sister of his wife, Mary. She had been living not far from Kensington at Campden House with her husband, Prince George of Denmark. They had hoped that their delicate son William, the only child who had survived from Anne's 17 pregnancies, would find the air salubrious. But it was not to be. William, who had been created Duke of Gloucester, died there at the age of 11 in 1700.

Anne moved into Kensington House with Prince George soon after her accession and though not a woman of many positive qualities, she soon set to work on the gardens and greatly extended them, employing Henry Wise (without George

* Presented to the British nation by the Kaiser Wilhelm II.

33

London), thus making him the most sought-after gardener in the country.

Anne had been on bad terms with William and her sister Mary for many years. The quarrels had been patched up, but Anne showed her feelings, perhaps, by having William's Dutch gardens uprooted. One of the reasons given was that she detested the smell of box which was used extensively in the parterres. She replaced them by a formal garden designed by Wise.

It must not be forgotten, however, that the one-time Sarah Jennings, now Duchess of Marlborough and the Queen's almost inseparable friend'* had become a very important person at court – Groom of the Stole, Keeper of the Privy Purse and Mistress of the Robes, all powerful and profitable appointments. Sarah had long hated William and might well have encouraged Anne to destroy William's gardens, for she was of a vindictive character.

Undoubtedly, the most important development was that the Queen enclosed no less than a hundred acres of Hyde Park to make a paddock for herds of deer and antelope and so, unwittingly, brought Kensington Gardens as we know them nearer.

The gravel pits behind the house were planted with trees and made into a much-admired garden. A beginning was also made with a sunken garden which has gradually developed into a major delight to visit. Nearby is the architectural triumph of Anne's improvements, the Orangery, designed by Hawksmoor and Vanbrugh. It is an immensely satisfying baroque building which has been refurbished in recent years and gracefully adorned within by Renaissance vases and statues from the Queen's gardens at Windsor. This 'stately Green House', as it was first described, was favoured by Anne as a 'Summer Supper House'. It is now used once more by members of the royal family who live in the palace, for small receptions and occasional concerts of chamber music or recitals.

Anne's last years brought her little happiness. Her husband George died in 1708 and was unlamented by the world as a useless drunkard. Her own health made her life increasingly wretched. It was said she suffered from gout, but it seems more likely that it was arthritis and by 1711 she was virtually crippled. Laudanum and brandy eased her pain and gambling provided her with some solace.

It was in 1711 that she finally broke with her friend Sarah after tempestuous quarrels which must have exhausted her. Fortunately Abigail Masham was there to give some comfort, even if this new friendship could never be more than a poor substitute for the joyous intimacies of the past.

* In their extraordinary correspondence over 20 years Anne was Mrs Morley, Sarah, Mrs Freeman. The Queen's letters are often full of mawkish affection and, at times, quite embarrassing expressions of love.

34

The Queen had a small carriage built in which she drove herself round the gardens and frequently the paddock, for she had been an enthusiastic huntress in the days of her youth. She often drove recklessly, probably half-dazed with laudanum, alcohol and worries about the succession.

Her father, James II, had died in France in 1701, leaving a son, James (b. 1688), by his second wife, Mary of Modena. A Tory faction had grown in power around Anne in her later years, plotting a Stuart and Catholic restoration backed by France. When it came to a power struggle, however, it was almost inevitable that the Protestant Whig grandees, beneficiaries of the 'Glorious Revolution' of 1688, should win. When Anne died in Kensington House on 1st August 1714, messengers had already been despatched to the Protestant George, Elector of Hanover.

Thus began the rule in Britain of the House of Hanover.

George I, who was 54, took a leisurely leave of his palace, Herrenhausen, in the land of Hanover which he had ruled for 16 years with a prudent moderation and kindness that had earned him genuine popularity. His departure was regretted.

Herrenhausen was delightful. Its grounds, like so many princely German gardens of the time, reflected in a more modest way the glories of Versailles with formal avenues lined with trees, statues of amorous fauns and dryads, fountains and waterfalls.

So pleasant was life there that neither of George's two mistresses wanted to leave – at first. Neither 'Madame' von Kielmansegge nor 'Madame' von Schulenberg was young or pretty. The first was of such ample proportions that she was soon irreverently called 'The Elephant' by the English. The second was very tall and thin so she was nicknamed 'The Maypole' until some wag decided that as Kielmansegge was 'The Elephant', Schulenberg must be 'The Castle'.*

Both were well rewarded by the King for their services in his new kingdom. Kielmansegge became Countess of Darlington and Leinster, while Schulenberg was created Duchess of Kendal and had a fine self-contained house built for her on the north side of what became in George's reign Kensington Palace.

England was never to see George's wife, the pretty Sophia Dorothea of Celle. In October 1694 she had been imprisoned in the Castle of Ahlden at the age of 28 and was to remain there for 32 years, known simply as the 'Princess of Ahlden'. Poor Sophia Dorothea, a direct ancestress of our royal family (her

---

* There is a charming public house in Holland Street, not far from Kensington Palace, called 'The Elephant and Castle'.

son was to be George II), had fallen madly in love with Philip von Konigsmarck, who was of a dangerously attractive family of aristocratic adventurers who came originally from Brandenburg. Philip's sister, the beautiful Aurora, became the mistress of Augustus of Saxony; his elder brother, Carl Johann, was a favourite of Charles II, but fled to escape hanging for the murder of Tom Thynne of Longleat.

Philip arrived at the court of Hanover and quickly charmed George who made him part of the court and a Colonel of Dragoons. Sophia Dorothea became infatuated, threw aside all restraint, committed adultery and was about to elope with him (and her jewels) whilst George was away in Berlin. The plans were betrayed at the last minute. Von Konigsmarck desperately fought with the guards who came to arrest him and in the struggle was killed, which was probably just as well for him.

When George came to Kensington with his German chamberlains, secretaries and negro servants,* his main interest there for years was to extend the house into a palace and embellish the main apartments. William Benson replaced Wren as the King's Surveyor (architect and builder), and William Kent, the talented protege of Lord Burlington, became his decorator and artist. Kent's most notable work was on the great staircase, including the fascinating trompe-l'oeil on the walls and his elegant ceilings in many of the state apartments. Fortunately they are there in good condition for the visitor of today to study.

As you look at the palace now it must be approximately as it was when George I's changes had been completed. There are those who dismiss it contemptuously as a rambling jumble of buildings put together without rhyme or reason and unworthy to be called a palace.

I find it immensely satisfying and very English. A Dutchman and a German may have given the commissions, but they had the services of Wren, Hawksmoor, Vanbrugh, Benson and Kent!

For years George left the gardens much as they were. He had a modest rectangular basin constructed where his turtles could swim until required for the royal soup. (This was roughly where the Round Pond is.) Nearby was a colony of edible snails (a 'snailery') to provide a further fresh delicacy when needed.

In Queen Anne's paddock the King kept a menagerie of tigers and civets. Although they were caged their smell and cries must have terrified the deer and antelope in the paddock. Perhaps, however, that was partly the reason for keeping them there.

The supply of sufficient water was becoming a problem. To

---

* They had been captured in his campaigns against the Turks when he led the 8,000-strong Hanoverian contingent in the Austrian Emperor's army.

How Hyde Park became 'The Park'

HYDE PARK HAD good reason to feel deprived during the 18th century as it saw Kensington Gardens basking in royal favour and receiving lavish grants. Not only were hundreds of acres sliced from it to make the gardens of the now upgraded 'Palace' of Kensington, there was precious little money left to maintain what remained in decent order.

It retained, however, one basic privilege which was to ensure a great future. Hyde Park stayed open to the public whilst Kensington Gardens were enclosed behind a sunken ha-ha and public access was occasional and restricted by class distinctions.

Some features of Hyde Park remained the same for many years. The hangings went on regularly at Tyburn, often attracting large crowds, especially if a well-known highwayman was to meet his end. Such a one was handsome John Maclean who had kept a grocer's shop locally and was popular in the taverns round the Park, especially with the girls, for he was a free-spender after a successful hold-up, perhaps on the Kensington or the Bayswater roads.

Tyburn's most memorable day, however, was 5th May 1760 when the fourth Earl Ferrers was hanged at the age of 40 for shooting his steward. After trial by his peers in Westminster Hall he had been sentenced to death. On the day appointed he left his quarters in the Tower of London and was driven in his own coach and six across the City to Tyburn. He wore a fine suit embroidered with silver and walked calmly enough to the gallows before a great crowd of spectators, many of whom had paid large sums for a vantage-point. In an ironic fashion this proved, I suppose, how much the English love a lord.

The Ring was no longer a parade-ground for fashion and beauty and was deserted long before its final decay and demolition. Nearby, however, 'honour' continued to claim its victims as the nobility and gentry fought their duels. In the reign of George III it is said there were nearly 200 with around 70 deaths, including three cases when both duellists were killed, thus leaving 'honour' doubly satisfied.

Opposite: The world-famous open forum, Speakers' Corner, Hyde Park.

43

There were military parades from time to time, continuing the tradition which has made the area north of the Serpentine to the Bayswater Road the British 'Champ de Mars'. During the reign of George III England was engaged in the protracted desperate struggle against Napoleon of which the outcome was long uncertain, and these parades were often a farewell to troops destined to fight and perhaps die in foreign fields.

By the end of the 18th century Mayfair was built right up to the eastern boundary of Hyde Park (Park Lane). To the north rows of houses were beginning to line the Bayswater Road.

By the 1820s Hyde Park had finally come into its own as 'The Park'. Belgravia had been built to the south-east of the Park and was beginning its inexorable progress westwards to Kensington. The north of Oxford Street had been developed and was moving along the Bayswater Road to Paddington.

London was steadily moving westwards and enterprising men such as Cubitt were building the great squares, crescents and streets on the fields and meadows that were owned by a few fortunate families such as the Grosvenors. It was a time when the wealth of England was increasing by leaps and bounds. The landed aristocracy and gentry benefited from improved agriculture and enclosures. Overseas trade was expanding, especially with the colonies, and the loss of America and the Napoleonic blockade were shrugged off with surprising ease. In the Midlands and North the Industrial Revolution got well under way in the second half of the 18th century, creating vast fortunes for a new class of men.

Hyde Park became a backdrop to the social scene for all classes in the 19th century. While coaches and carriages would slowly progress along the perimeter roads, riders would show off the paces of their horses in Rotten Row. At the same time the Park was still regularly used for drill and band practice by the Guards Regiments stationed in nearby Wellington Barracks such as these Scots Guards shown crossing Rotten Row in 1893.

On those acres, which had been mostly fields for market gardeners and graziers, virtually a new educational and cultural quarter was created: The Royal Albert Hall, the Royal College of Music, the Royal College of Art, the Imperial College of Science and Technology, the Royal School of Mines, the Science Museum, the Natural History Museum, the Victoria and Albert Museum.

It is an astonishing heritage inspired by a young German Prince of the House of Saxe-Coburg and Gotha.

Albert believed that men and women should be educated in the exciting fields of new knowledge to benefit themselves and the nation. He believed that they should at the same time enrich their lives with music and art. He also believed in a synthesis that would produce harmonious personalities, enjoying productive work and creative leisure.

All that sounds rather Germanic. It sounded very Germanic to politicians such as Palmerston and the fox-hunting squirearchy who saw no need to spread education, especially at State expense.

But Albert, as Victoria sensed, knew the way forward, in spite of the ignorant Philistines who opposed him. Spare a thought for him and remember his legacy to a country where he

The Great Exhibition: the transept looking south. The designer of the Crystal Palace, Joseph Paxton, was compelled to make one major alteration to his original plans. He had to provide an arched transept in the centre of the building large enough to cover two giant elms in the middle of the proposed site.

56

An artist's impression of the Central Hall of Arts and Sciences, known to future generations as the Royal Albert Hall.

remained for the most part unpopular, as you walk among the trees and flowers in Hyde Park and Kensington Gardens or glimpse his Memorial as you come out from a Promenade concert in the Albert Hall, or even just pass in a car that is well-designed.

Grace and Favour in Kensington Gardens

IN COMPARISON WITH Hyde Park, where so many exciting events took place, Kensington Gardens slumbered peacefully for several decades after the death of George II in 1760, within the framework of the gardens created by his wife, Caroline.

The 19th century brought an awakening, but it was 'genteel', as befitted an area to be long associated with gentility. By now the Gardens were opened daily to the 'respectably-dressed', with all that this implied in the way of class distinction. Queen Caroline's Mount was levelled; the ha-ha dividing the Gardens from the Park was gradually, over a long period, filled in. Ornamental trees and shrubs were planted on the west bank of the Long Water and most important of all, in the south of the Gardens a beginning was made with the Flower Walk which stretches for nearly a mile in a straight line and was destined to become one of the sights of London.

Flocks of sheep were brought in to keep the grass short and helped to provide an atmosphere of almost rural tranquillity right up to the beginning of the Second World War in 1939.

The wealth of Victorian England was increasing at such a phenomenal rate that it was not long before the developers ran out of building sites round Hyde Park and moved westwards to the environs of Kensington Gardens.

A significant venture of the 1840s was the leasing of land on the western boundary of the palace for the building of a number of what were called 'villas'. It was, no doubt, a correct, classical description at the time, but do not think that these 'villas' were the modest suburban homes of today; they are the large mansions of Kensington Palace Gardens – a very grand private road, lined with noble trees, which also gives access to the palace. These mansions are now for the most part embassies, some of which have been rebuilt in a not unpleasing Lutyens style. The Russians have for long occupied several at the Bayswater end and these have been left as they were built, imposing examples of early Victorian architecture with a French flavour. The mansion where receptions are given by the Russians has a very large

Kensington Palace as it is today.

59

salon at the back with tall French windows looking on to part of the gardens of Kensington Palace, where several members of the royal family live in very grand apartments.

The 'villas' of Kensington Palace Gardens brought a new community of rich tenants who soon pressed for and obtained special privileges, such as private entrances to the Gardens. In time this fortunately led to the replacement of the old walls with open iron railings.

It was not long before the development of Kensington in the south and along the Bayswater Road in the north was in full swing – every year saw new squares, terraces and crescents, and shopping areas to serve them sprang up along Kensington High Street and in Notting Hill Gate.

Those who came to live in the new areas were probably for the most part not as aristocratic or influential as those dwelling in Mayfair or Belgravia, but they were often more interesting.

Successful artists, musicians and writers settled in Kensington, creating social circles which set a certain 'tone'. They had close links with a growing rentier class whose members, both men and women, were often of high culture. They spent their leisure reading and visiting galleries, museums and concerts. They had the means to travel widely, often with the new facilities offered by Thomas Cook, the pioneer of tourism, and returned home with minds broadened and much to discuss.

There were also those, often of humble origin, who had made their 'pile' in the colonies and America and came back to enjoy the fruits of their luck and labour. They had the money to build vast mansions, some of which still stand, converted into hotels or flats, and spent extravagantly to secure a foothold in 'society'. Ostracised at first, their wealth soon made them welcome, especially if they had sons and daughters of marriageable age whose financial prospects endeared them to hard-pressed mothers looking to the future for their offspring.

Marriages in those days meant children: large families were a characteristic of the Victorian age. For the upper classes living around Kensington and Bayswater the Gardens provided an excellent open space where nannies, nursemaids – at times, even mothers – could parade the well-nurtured children in perambulators and later watch over their play, especially near the Round Pond where the pastime of sailing model boats took place.

Kensington Gardens has in fact run the risk of becoming identified with children to the point of mawkishness. By the Long Water is the almost venerated statue of Peter Pan, Barrie's boy who would never grow up, standing on a pedestal decorated with squirrels, rabbits and mice. Over in the children's playground is the Elfin Oak, a stump from Richmond Park, carved by Ivor Innes in the thirties with fairies and elves and pet animals. After the war it was in a sad state, but Spike Milligan organised funds to have it renovated.

60

There has always been, however, another side to Kensington Gardens. For example, Matthew Arnold, poet, man of letters, high-minded public servant, bitter critic of the Philistinism around him, embodied much that was best in the Victorian era and he has left us his 'Lines Written In Kensington Gardens', published in 1852, when he was 30. Here are a few of the lines:

'Birds here make song, each bird has his,
Across the girdling city's hum.
How green under the boughs it is!
How thick the tremulous sheep-cries come!

Sometimes a child will cross the glade
To take his nurse his broken toy;
Sometimes a thrush flits overhead
Deep in her unknown day's employ.

Calm soul of all things! make it mine
To feel, amid the city's jar,
That there abides a peace of thine,
Man did not make, and cannot mar.'

The popular pastime of sailing model boats on the Round Pond in Kensington Gardens, an illustration from *The Graphic*, August 1874.

In the early 1950s the Dutch elm disease began to take its toll in the Gardens, and in 1953 the full extent of the disaster became public knowledge. The great avenues of elms planted for Queen Caroline in the early 18th century to frame the Broad Walk from Bayswater Road to Kensington Gore were to be felled in their entirety, partly because they were diseased, partly because age had made them dangerous.

There was a public outcry, letters to *The Times* and so on, but the arguments of the experts were irrefutable. The trees came down and left a gap not only in the Gardens, but in the hearts of many. The Gardens looked naked and ashamed. Replacement saplings of maples and limes were planted. During a walk on Easter Monday, 1984, I noticed that at last the saplings had become trees and the trees had become an avenue.

In spite of the second outbreak of disease in the '70s which killed all but one elm in the Gardens, there happily remained enough great trees of other species to provide a covering screen, and on this day their outlines were softened into a misty cloud of pale green as the leaves came to life in the sunshine.

In Victorian and Edwardian days the Flower Walk was a fashionable parade, especially on Sundays after church. Even between the wars there was still a certain distinction in being seen there.

As fashion departed, however, those who frequented the Walk as a haven of peace and beauty were the happier. There is a path turning off left as you approach Palace Gate which can lead you to some of the greatest pleasures the Gardens have to give. On your right you first pass a series of set pieces which,

The recently-restored Queen's Temple near the Long Water.

whatever the budget cuts, always seem to be fresh and imaginative. The path then meanders round to a fine side view of the Albert Memorial, and if you are there in the early months of the year there are clusters of snowdrops and crocuses flowering in the lush grass near your feet to tell you that the worst of winter is over (I am afraid not always the truth).

The great showpiece of the year there, however, is (depending on the weather) between late March and the first weeks of April when 'a crowd, a host of golden daffodils . . . fluttering and dancing in the breeze', covers the lawns and the raised banks that form a protective barrier between the Gardens and the Kensington road.

What is more, to give some variety, the daffodils are now massed alternately with narcissi along the banks.

Facing the Round Pond and framed by the row of great yews in front of the palace is a statue of Victoria as she was at the time of her accession, sculpted by her talented daughter, Princess Louise. It was placed in the Gardens when a fund was raised for this purpose by the residents of Kensington at the time of the Golden Jubilee in 1887, fifty years on.

Now the palace once more plays a significant rôle in the life of the royal family. Prince Charles and Princess Diana hold modest court there, in the style that pleases them. With them are their sons, Prince William and Prince Henry.

Kensington Gardens is now once more part of the environment of future generations of kings and queens.

Model yacht sailing on the Round Pond is still as popular today as it was in Victorian times.

A Near Disaster

The great royal firework display in Hyde Park on the evening of 28th July 1981 to herald the marriage next day in St Paul's Cathedral of the Prince of Wales and Lady Diana Spencer only narrowly avoided turning into a disaster on a national scale. As it was, 1,000 were hurt and 100 needed hospital treatment after the vast crowd of 750,000, far larger than anyone expected, pressed to leave at the end of the show and found the Park gates locked. Fortunately the crowd was in a good-humoured, holiday mood and was patient. But the effect of even a slow pressure by such vast numbers is as irresistible as the tide. If one small incident had sparked off a panic, the result does not bear thinking about.

As it happened, not much was made of the story, as the media had for weeks been working up a frenzy of national rejoicing and no one wanted to spoil the wedding day of the popular heir to the throne and his attractive bride.

Thoughts of what might have happened, however, still recur like nightmares to those in charge. Understandably, the gates had been closed when it was realised the Park was filled to capacity. But, somewhere along the line, there was a failure to ensure that officials were on duty to unlock these gates in good time.

For Hyde Park it was the greatest spectacular ever seen; there was a greater concentration of royalty, heads of state, diplomats and dignitaries in the special stands than the Park had probably witnessed over four centuries. They were driven in coaches from Buckingham Palace where the Queen had given a dinner for the wedding guests who had come from all over the world.

Shortly after, the Prince of Wales arrived with his mother, the Queen and his father, Prince Philip, but without his bride Diana for she was spending the evening in seclusion, though the venue, Clarence House, the home of the Queen Mother, was near enough for her to hear the bangs and watch the rockets.

Whilst royalty and its guests had been making their way to their seats the crowds had been entertained by a display of searchlights criss-crossing the sky to the strains of cheerful music relayed through amplifiers.

To add to the general feeling of well-being, after days of doubtful weather, the evening was fine.

Now it was time for Prince Charles to step forward and receive a flaming torch from a charming disabled girl and then light a fuse which set fire to the beacon in front of the palace of canvas and scaffolding (300 ft long, 40 ft high) which was the centrepiece of the display.

As the beacon leapt into flame the news was flashed from the Post Office Tower, a notable London landmark, to Windsor so that the next beacon could be lit. The message was passed on and on so that by 11 p.m. more than 100 beacons were flaming in the skies all over Britain.

By now the batteries of television cameras in Hyde Park were transmitting the brilliant scene to millions in Britain, Canada, Australia, the USA and elsewhere.

The Prince Regent would have turned in his grave had he been able to compare such a huge world-wide audience with the London crowds, large as they were, who had witnessed his splendid coronation festivities in this same Park. He could, however, have comforted himself with the thought that it was all still in the family.

Once the beacon which Prince Charles had lit was ablaze the firework display erupted into the sky with mortars, rockets and fountains of light in continually changing patterns of colour. It was a great show for there were 12,000 items, containing two and a half tons of explosives, and they had cost £25,000, defrayed from the sale of 100,000 programmes at £1 apiece (the balance went to a fund for the disabled).

The set pieces arranged around the canvas palace were rather sedate – elaborate royal coat of arms and the badges of the regiments of which Prince Charles is Colonel-in-chief – but the finale had the crowds ooing and ahing with pleasure, for it was a giant Catherine wheel, 35 ft across, with the initials C and D blazing into the night.

The Park recovered, but the events of the evening, hopefully, make it unlikely that such numbers would ever be allowed inside again. There had been officials against using the Park for the firework display, but they had been overruled by those in favour of mounting 'the greatest spectacular ever' for the royal wedding.

To control safely crowds of such a size as came that evening there would have to be an elaborate system of high steel barriers breaking up the Park into a series of compartments separated by corridors patrolled by police. One development would lead to another. Commercialisation 'to make the Royal Parks pay their way' would soon be the parrot-cry, marking the beginning of the end of a great heritage.

St James's Park

IF YOU STAND facing Horse Guards Parade with St James's Park behind you, you will be at the heart of the life of the nation. The Old Admiralty will be to your left, Downing Street, where the Prime Minister and Chancellor of the Exchequer live and work, to your right and beyond, the clock-tower of Big Ben presides over the Palace of Westminster where Parliament sits.

As you turn into the Park you will see the statue of Earl Mountbatten of Burma, unveiled by the Queen on 2nd November 1983. It is a modest-looking statue on a low plinth of that legendary man – war-hero, last Viceroy of India, First Sea Lord, uncle of Prince Philip, adviser to the Queen and her family – who was blown up by the IRA on 27th August 1979 whilst on holiday at his Irish castle.

St James's Park is by far the most prestigious and in many ways the most romantically beautiful of the Royal Parks. Small though it is – only 52 acres if the surrounding roads are excluded – St James's symbolises much of the English tradition. Its visitors experience the majesty of the historic buildings surrounding it, and take great pleasure in strolling its avenues of trees, lawns and set flower-beds.

It owes its existence to Henry VIII, a wicked tyrant who has in some extraordinary way been presented to later generations as a jolly, hearty monarch, typically English in outlook. In fact he was descended from the Welshman Owen Tudor and Katherine, the French Princess who was the widow of Henry V of Agincourt renown.

There is no doubt, however, that the Tudor sovereigns were very able and Henry VIII was one of the ablest. He had great energy, was a good scholar and a discerning patron of the arts. He was also cruel and an arch-dissembler. You could call him our own Renaissance Prince.

He had some influence on the development of most of the Royal Parks. Unfortunately, scarcely a trace remains of his most ambitious creation, the great Palace of Nonsuch, south of London, with a 1,700 acre deer park and gardens as splendid as

The Horse Guards from St James's Park in the time of Charles II.

any in Europe at the time. The entire estate was given in the next (17th) century to Charles II's most rapacious mistress, Barbara Villiers, later Duchess of Cleveland, who had the Palace demolished and the land sold off.

In November 1529 Henry VIII was rowed from Greenwich Palace, which had become the family home of the Tudor dynasty, landed at Whitehall and took possession of York Place, the recently vacated palace of the now disgraced Cardinal Wolsey, who for years had administered the realm for his master and himself with profitable efficiency. Wolsey was Archbishop of York and York Place was his official dwelling. The Cardinal had made it a splendid Palace, magnificently appointed. Soon after the King took it over the name was changed to Whitehall to help erase the memory of Wolsey. Henry almost immediately set in hand great extensions, but at the same time felt the need for a smaller, more private dwelling nearby where he could relax away from the official, inquisitive, gossiping life of the court.

It is difficult for us now to imagine that, in the time of Henry VIII, across the road from the Palace of Whitehall where we are accustomed to imposing buildings and splendid gardens, the King's view would have been very different. All he would have seen were marshy fields and meandering streams set among trees, mainly oaks, the survivors of the great forest that once covered the land.

The fields belonged to a medieval hospice of St James the Lesser, near Charing Cross, in which the Church had for generations given shelter to a small community of leper sisters who diligently tilled the land.

Henry decided that this estate on his doorstep, so to speak, was just what he wanted. So he took over the 160 acre site, which was administered by Eton College, and gave in exchange land in East Anglia. To round off the property the King also took over 100 acres from Westminster Abbey with compensation of farmland in Berkshire.

The Palace of St James's which Henry built on his new estate is, as we can see today, of modest proportions. The gatehouse which faces north up St James's Street towards Piccadilly is decorated with the Tudor rose and crown, and the initials H for Henry and A for Anne Boleyn.

It is not too fanciful to think that Henry's decision to buy the estate had been largely inspired by his infatuation for Anne and his desire to share with her a retreat, a love-nest, where they could be happy in comparative privacy.

Below: Two old views of St James's Park, about 1680. St James's Park was transformed by Charles II who had a canal dug from the Whitehall end to the Mulberry Garden where Buckingham Palace was to be built in a later century. He was the first monarch to open the Park to the public and regularly walked here with his courtiers and spaniels.

A garden, orchard and avenue of trees were laid out alongside the palace to enhance the scene.

The Tudor gardens of royalty and nobility had by now often copied the French rectangular arrangement: straight paths separated the quite small flower-beds which were protected by low wooden rails painted in green and white. In the beds were low hedges of box and yew to set off the flowers that bloomed in season from early spring – crocuses, primroses, violets, hyacinths, daffodils, wallflowers and marigolds. But already the joy of the English garden was the rose which would flower for months, and perhaps produce even a Christmas bloom.

Lilac and honeysuckle scented the trellised arbours and the orchard blossomed with almond, peach, cherry, apple and pear.

Beyond the new palace and its gardens the entire estate was surrounded by a fine brick wall, making St James's the first of the London Royal Parks to be enclosed. There were fish and water-fowl in the Tyburn and other streams which flowed into Cowford Pool and Rosamond's Pond. A herd of deer was kept for hunting, more to provide venison for the royal table than for the limited exercise afforded by those acres. Henry enjoyed shooting the deer for he had the reputation of being one of the best archers in the land (probably by now with the cross-bow rather than the longbow).

In the area of what is now the Horse Guards Parade and its surrounding official buildings Henry had what might be called a recreational centre made for himself. There was a cockpit, a tennis court, a bowling green and a tiltyard (an exercise ground for mounted men). Henry liked to have a tiltyard near his homes for in his youth he was a fine horseman with a good eye and a strong arm, and he enjoyed showing his prowess at charging with a lance to carry off the suspended iron ring.

In a few years Henry had thus created out of the lonely fields of the leper sisters an enclave of princely pleasure, self-contained and reasonably private, yet within a few yards of the great rambling official Palace of Whitehall and not far from the ancient Palace of Westminster, which had been now given over almost entirely to the judiciary, the lawyers and the clerks of the Exchequer.

Henry's park of pleasure was, however, created against a backcloth of increasing tragedy and terror. Wolsey was succeeded by Thomas Cromwell as the King's minister and proved the truth of the contemporary saying, 'Un inglese italianizzato è il diabolo incarnato', ('An Englishman

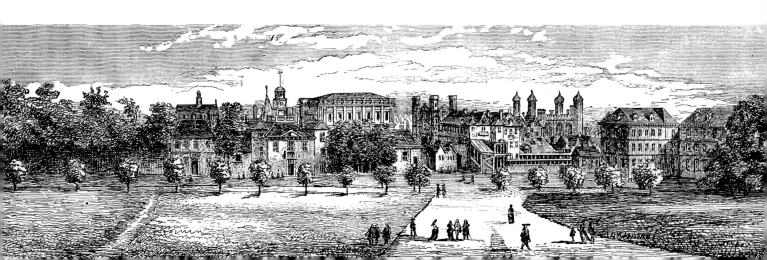

italianised is the devil incarnate'). The King's divorce from Katherine of Aragon was decreed by servile English bishops even though it led to the fateful break with Rome and the enmity of the powerful Emperor Charles V, the Queen's nephew. Anne Boleyn, who had resolutely held out for marriage, was installed as Queen and in 1533 was crowned in Westminster Abbey by the Archbishop of Canterbury and walked in a splendid procession along Whitehall under a canopy borne by the Barons of the Cinque Ports. As we read in Shakespeare's *Henry VIII* . . . 'she is an angel; Our King has all the Indies in his arms, And more and richer, when he strains that lady; I cannot blame his conscience.'

Anne had not long, however, to enjoy the pleasures of St James's. There was little time for her to see the garden bloom and the orchard blossom; little time for laughter and caresses against the background of sweet voices singing to the lute and viol.

Within three years (in 1536) she was imprisoned in the Tower, found guilty of absurd sexual infidelities and beheaded. It is difficult to believe that even Henry could afterwards enjoy his park of pleasure in the same way, for in killing Anne he had probably killed his only love.

Anne was succeeded as Queen by Jane Seymour who died in childbirth after giving Henry the son he wanted so desperately to ensure the future of the dynasty. The son, however, after reigning for six years as Edward VI died at the age of 16 and was succeeded by Mary ('Bloody' Mary), the daughter of Katherine of Aragon and resolute in the Catholic faith, whose reign also lasted no more than six years. She had married Philip II of Spain, but there were no children. If there had been, the future of England would probably have been no more than as a Catholic province of a Hapsburg Empire. On Mary's death, however, Anne's daughter, Elizabeth, reigned gloriously for 44 years, covering one of the most memorable epochs in British history and thus avenging the savage death of her mother.

With Elizabeth the Tudor dynasty came to an end. Henry VIII's sister, Margaret, had married the Stuart King of Scotland, James IV. Their granddaughter, Mary, Queen of Scots, beheaded in England by Queen Elizabeth for plotting her overthrow, had a son, James VI of Scotland. On the death of Elizabeth it was he who in 1603 succeeded to the English throne as James I.

An unpleasant, slobbering pederast, he nevertheless left his mark on St James's Park. The possession of a menagerie of exotic animals had at this time become increasingly a prestige symbol among princes, especially as exploration, trade and conquest were opening up the world.

James acquired some crocodiles and kept them in ponds in the Park, not far from the palace, probably roughly where the

70

that the Mollet family, who were very distinguished royal gardeners in France of the school of Le Notre, played a part in developing St James's. Gabriel and André held official posts there as gardeners between 1661 and 1664.

It is also on record that an eminent French gardener, whether Le Nôtre or a Mollet, who viewed the Park when Charles had had the initial work done, advised the King strongly against further changes, concluding 'that its native Beauty, Country Air and Deserts had something greater in them than anything he could contrive'.

The French of the age of Louis XIV, 'the Sun King', are often accused of intellectual and artistic arrogance (they had good cause!) so that it is pleasant to record that it was one of them who recognised that the classical French garden would not suit the English temperament. What is more, he was right!

So the acres between the avenues were left as meadows in which small herds of deer and cows roamed while ducks and other wild-fowl swam in the canal.

Charles had become an enthusiastic player of Pall Mall (Paille Maille) in France where it was fashionable at court. Florentine in origin (Pallamaglio, Ball and Mallet), it was a more strenuous form of croquet, played in a court several hundred yards long, fenced with a palisade. The King had a court laid out at first in what is now Pall Mall. Soon, however, the area started to be built on and with increasing traffic and disturbance the King had a new, improved court laid out along the Mall inside the Park. A Keeper of the Pell Mell described to Pepys that the surface of the court was made of cockleshells, ground into a powder and 'spread to keep it fast'.

Away on the other side of the Park was Birdcage Walk about which there is a certain mystery. On the one hand there seems little doubt that there were aviaries and also cages for exotic wild animals. The Keeper of the King's Birds was a certain Edward Storey whose lodge is said to have stood by the present entrance of Storey's Gate. Yet contemporary prints do not show any such structures.

In this area there were also preserved some decoy ponds to trap wild birds. They seem to have been there since Tudor times.

Horse Guards Parade also began to take on its present rôle for it became a mustering-ground for the four regiments of Household Cavalry raised for the protection of the King's person.

This then was the background, simple compared with that of Versailles, in which Charles II strolled with his courtiers and spaniels to take the air.

It was an astonishing episode in the life of the Park, never to be repeated. Here was a King, returned from long, tedious years of exile to a country that still harboured desperate men who had reason to hate the monarchy, walking without guards in the centre of London, feeding the ducks, greeting perhaps his Queen, perhaps one of his mistresses – and, what is more, visible, even approachable to all, for he had opened the Park to the public.

In all this Charles showed great courage, but it was matched with equal cunning. His promenades in St James's Park, like his dining, wining and gambling before onlookers in the galleries at the Palace of Whitehall, owed something to the semi-public appearances of Louis XIV, but more to his determination to establish himself in the minds of the English as an easy-going, affable, pleasure-loving King who was not over-interested in the politics of the day.

Nothing could have been further from the truth. His loyalties lay more with France than with England. His mother was French; he was a grandson of Henri Quatre; he admired the grandeur of Louis XIV who was achieving ascendancy over Europe politically, militarily and culturally. But Charles, in addition to all this, was base enough to accept large subsidies from Louis (as well as a witty, good-looking mistress to join his harem, Louise de la Kerouaille), contrived that England should join France in a humiliating war against the Dutch and ruled the country for the last four years of his reign without a Parliament.

The most dangerous treachery, however, was that he was a secret Catholic who plotted with the help of the French King to restore England to the old faith.

Nevertheless, what would be called today his 'public relations exercise' succeeded brilliantly, for his popular image is secure in history as a King of great charm who liked the ladies and widened the aristocracy by granting dukedoms to his sons by them.

One of his more agreeable mistresses, the actress Nell Gwynne, (their son was created Duke of St Albans), had a house in Pall Mall with a garden at the back facing the Mall and the Park. One day she was in her garden looking out over the wall when the King came along with John Evelyn, who has left a diary of the period. He recorded with sorrow that Nell began what was clearly a bawdy conversation with the King and that he replied in kind.

I have always enjoyed that anecdote for although I know Evelyn is an important, almost eminent figure, he was more than a little pompous. His family had become very rich through the manufacture of gunpowder but on the outbreak of the Civil War, Evelyn, a fervent royalist, explained to Charles I that he could not join him as it would ruin him financially. He then went abroad on an extended tour of Italy and France to appreciate the works of art with cool detachment, while his King was defeated and finally executed.

What probably annoyed Evelyn was that Nell, 'an impudent

Following page: View of St James's Park and Buckingham House, published in 1763, the year after George III acquired the house. It shows clearly the canal – 2,800 feet long and 120 feet wide – created by Charles II, which in the early 19th century was transformed by the Prince Regent's architect John Nash into the sinuous, irregularly-shaped lake we see today.

77

comedian', interrupted him just as he was presenting the King with 'some sheets of History'.

On this walk Charles might well have continued along the Mall with its avenues of young elms and limes, past the pheasantry where Marlborough House now stands, past St James's Palace and its gardens, and then looked towards the Mulberry Garden and Goring House. This was now the home of Henry Bennet, later Earl of Arlington, the King's Lord Chamberlain and minister, who was certainly privy to the dangerous knowledge that Charles was a secret Roman Catholic and a pensioner of Louis XIV.

You could say that Arlington as an arch-dissembler was in the class of his master. He was a secret Roman Catholic himself and was impeached by Parliament in 1674 for popery, embezzlement and betrayal of trust. His cunning wits enabled him to extricate himself and when Goring House burned down he was rich enough from his public offices to rebuild it in splendid style, with stabling for forty or more horses, including a dozen hunters. He renamed it Arlington House, another ancestor of Buckingham Palace.

To return to the promenade of Charles, he might well then have turned left, passed the western end of the canal and stayed to look at the caged animals and aviaries in Birdcage Walk before sauntering back to Whitehall.

In winter when the canal froze there was for London a novel activity – skating ('sliding' they called it) which Charles and his brother, then Duke of York (later James II) had brought over from Holland where they had also spent some time during their years of exile.

To sum up this Restoration Park of Charles II, Pepys has good, middle-class low-key comment: 'My wife come to me to Whitehall, and we went and walked a good while in St James's Parke (sic) to see the brave alterations.' In fact the King had created a revolutionary new Royal Park in the centre of London.

Charles died in 1685. His brother, James II, after a troublesome three years' reign during which he attempted to bring back authoritarian rule and the Roman Catholic religion, was forced to flee in 1688 when the Protestant Prince William of Orange had successfully landed with an army at the invitation of the British Establishment. Yet William's links with the Stuarts were very close indeed. His mother, Mary, was a sister of Charles II and James II. His wife, Mary, was daughter of James II by his first wife, Anne Hyde.

William and Mary reigned jointly and successfully. They had little impact on St James's, putting their considerable energies into other Royal Parks. William did, however, build a small retreat on Duck Island where he could drink tea or wine with his intimates, nearly all Dutchmen who had come over with him. Mary died in 1694 and William in 1702. Mary's sister succeeded as Queen Anne, and was the last of the Stuart monarchs.

In 1698 the Palace of Whitehall had been almost entirely burned down and was not rebuilt, partially because King William had always disliked it, partially because of the cost. The relatively small St James's Palace built by Henry VIII as a cosy retreat became from now on the official residence of the court of an increasingly important world power.

Queen Anne ensured that the Park was looked after, employing Henry Wise already mentioned in the section on Kensington Gardens.

The main structural change to the Park during her reign, however, was made by a very attractive grandee of the time, John Sheffield (1648–1721), Earl of Mulgrave by inheritance, created Duke of Buckingham by Anne. He acquired Arlington House, pulled it down and built a splendid, medium-sized palace on the site, renamed it Buckingham House, and thus gave the 'Buckingham' part to the present palace.

Sheffield, soldier, sailor, poet, patron of literature, was a favourite at the court of both Charles II and James II. He was bold enough to raise his eyes to Anne, who was seventeen at the time. Charles was angered at his presumption, stripped him of his lucrative places and banished him from court. He was, however, soon back in favour! When Anne came to the throne twenty years later she showed that his attentions had not been unwelcome. He was given office, a handsome pension, as well as the dukedom. When he was building Buckingham House he decided he needed an extra slice of adjoining Crown land to complete his plans. Anne was at first reluctant to grant his wishes, but finally succumbed to his charm.

Sheffield was now in a position to align his new mansion so that the vistas of the Mall and the canal with their avenues of trees converged on his open forecourt, embellished with a decorative fountain in the Italian style. With superb panache, he had created the impression that St James's Park had been designed for his benefit.

In time the royal family became increasingly aware of the attractions of the site of Buckingham House. The property eventually passed to an illegitimate son of Sheffield, who was made to realise there were serious flaws in his father's title to the land and that the lease had not many years to run. He was offered generous terms by the Crown and accepted them so that in 1762 George III, a year after his coronation and marriage to Charlotte of Mecklenburg-Strelitz, acquired Buckingham House and its grounds. The ostensible motive was to provide a Dower House for the Queen, but George and Charlotte made it their home. Their eldest son, the future Prince Regent and George IV, had been born at St James's Palace, but in 'The

Opposite: Buckingham House, which was acquired by George III in 1762, a year after his coronation and marriage to Charlotte of Mecklenburg-Strelitz.

80

Opposite: The Duke of York Monument at Carlton House Terrace.

on the east and the new Buckingham Palace rising on the west.

The fine, mature avenues of trees were preserved on the boundaries and as far as possible within the Park. New plantations were created. Paths were contoured round the lake and shrubs planted, though it was not until later that the flower-beds brought colour to the scene, varied according to season.

Islands were created on the lake to increase the atmosphere of 'natural' beauty and two are still there, one at each end. The one by the Horse Guards retained the old name of Duck Island, though it is in fact connected to the Park.

The bridge Nash had built lasted until 1857 when it was replaced by one of those elegant iron structures that the Victorians designed so well. After the last war, however, it began to deteriorate and was replaced in 1957 by a concrete bridge designed by Eric Bedford which is not as attractive, but does provide splendid views, particularly east and west.

With the earth excavated to form the lake Nash built up a terrace on the north side from Marlborough House to the Trafalgar Square end. This enabled the impressive Carlton House Terrace to be developed, broken by the Duke of York's steps and Waterloo Place beyond. That had been the site of the Prince Regent's luxurious Carlton House which was demolished in 1831.

Nothing, however, came of the plan to develop the south side beyond Birdcage Walk.

Instead, Wellington Barracks was built to house a battalion of the Foot Guards. Alongside is the Guards' Chapel, now rebuilt after its destruction by a flying bomb during a service on Sunday 18th June 1944 which caused many deaths in the congregation of nearly 200.

Further along towards Storey's Gate and Westminster the charming 18th-century houses in Queen Anne's Gate which on one side back on to Birdcage Walk were, fortunately, left alone, together with a statue of the Queen of that name in Garter robes set into one of the walls.

By the 1830s Nash's grand project had been largely realised. George IV died in 1830, without seeing Buckingham Palace completed, and was succeeded by his brother, the Duke of

Below: Nash's new plan for St James's Park, showing the transformation of the canal into the far more interesting lake seen today.

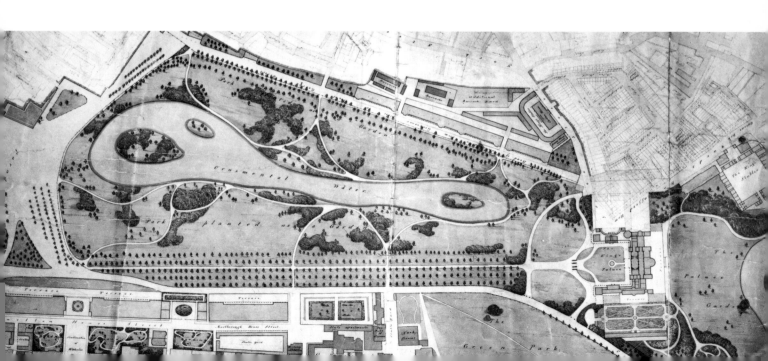

Clarence, as William IV. He was a man of modest tastes and had no wish to live in the new palace, which he thought an absurd extravagance, preferring to continue living at Clarence House (which Nash had also built) and using the adjoining St James's Palace for court functions.

Undoubtedly, however, the climax of the whole Nash plan for the area was reached in July 1837 when Queen Victoria, aged 18, drove through the great Marble Arch* into the open courtyard of Buckingham Palace as its first mistress.

After the death of her uncle, William IV, she had succeeded to the throne on 20th June and could not wait to leave the apartment in Kensington Palace she had shared unwillingly with her mother, the Duchess of Kent.

Nash did not live to see that day. He had died, aged 83, in 1835 on the Isle of Wight at East Cowes Castle, the grand home he had built for himself at the turn of the century.

In any case when George IV had died in 1830, public and Parliamentary disquiet over the escalating (and unauthorised) costs of the new palace led to Nash's dismissal and searching and humiliating appearances before Select Committees which, however, did not find him guilty of personal dishonesty. He had always had more than a normal share of envious detractors.

Nash has, however, had the last say. His work is now recognised as part of the national heritage. St James's Park is a thriving example of Nash's genius, constantly renewed by those who care for it.

The Park enjoyed a remarkable degree of popularity for many years, which more than compensated for the inevitable and proper criticism of detail from time to time.

In 1840 the Ornithological Society was given permission to build a cottage on Duck Island and later an aviary and two boathouses were added.†

The facade of the palace was radically changed in 1847 when Parliament voted funds for a new east wing which provided more rooms. Prince Albert probably had another reason for wanting the new wing: it would screen off the main entrance and satisfy his obsessive desire for privacy. More by luck than judgment the new front included the first-floor balcony from which the royal family has so often greeted the crowds of loyal subjects below, mainly on occasions of celebration.

The Park did, however, suffer a considerable loss of ground and amenity when the vast Queen Victoria Memorial, on its island site, and the surrounding crescent-shaped gardens were

* Long relegated now to an absurd island site at the north-eastern end of Hyde Park.

† A century later during the 1939–45 war the lake was drained to prevent it being used by enemy bombers as a guide. Temporary government offices were built in the Park.

set in place before the palace in 1911. The lake had to be shortened and over 100 fine trees were felled.

The concept, however, is so successful, even if extravagantly grandiose in the Edwardian style, with the statue of the Queen embellished with gilded figures of Victory, Courage and Constancy, that it gives an appropriate splendour to the spectacle of Palace, Mall, Park and the surrounding buildings.

It was well that this triumphant, self-confident memorial to the Victorian era and British imperial power was put up three years before the outbreak of the 1914–18 war. After 1918 European civilisation was totally changed and events led, almost inexorably, to the 1939–45 war which brought to Britain both victory and the end of Empire and hegemony.

The flower-beds of these gardens, with the theme predominantly scarlet, are one of the great showpieces for the gardeners of the central Royal Parks. They have to be as near perfection as possible for they are constantly on view to the Queen, Prince Philip and the high officers of the Court. On the occasion of a state visit when Kings, Queens and Presidents drive down the Mall to the Palace, the gardens become almost a national source of pride.

The Mall became, as Nash had hoped, a triumphal way when the Admiralty Arch was built in 1910, linking Trafalgar Square and beyond to the Mall and St James's Park complex.

Over the years there have been many necessary additions to the Park – more seating, including deck chairs, a playground, public conveniences and signposts. Litter is a constant problem, only partially solved by bins.

Our survey of St James's Park ends with a brief note on the Chapel Royal of St James's Palace. It is a very elegant structure, built by Inigo Jones for Charles I who wanted his French wife, Henrietta Maria, a fervent Catholic, to have a chapel where she could worship according to her religion.

Until this century the Chapel Royal has been the scene of most of the great royal marriages which were virtually conducted in private, with only close relatives present.

Queen Mary married Prince George there in 1893. Victoria married Prince Albert there. The Prince Regent, later George IV, married the disastrous Caroline of Brunswick there. The list is long and illustrious, back to the daughter of Charles I and Henrietta Maria who married the Prince of Orange there in 1641.

The chapel is now much altered but a magnificent painted ceiling, which some have attributed to Holbein, survives. It is still possible to attend morning service here on certain Sundays in the year and at Epiphany royal gifts of gold, frankincense and myrrh are traditionally offered.

The Green Park

WITH THE BEST will in the world, there is little to enthuse about in this almost featureless Royal Park of 51 acres, set in a magnificent site between Piccadilly and Constitution Hill, with Buckingham Palace and the Victoria Memorial Gardens beyond, and at its eastern boundary, the Queen's Walk running down from the Ritz Hotel to Lancaster House in the Mall.

Nothing, but nothing has happened there for a long time. The Green Park has, however, had its great days when the paths were frequented by fashion and beauty; it was the scene of two spectacular disasters; assassins have lurked among the trees waiting to shoot at royalty driving to or from the Palace.

For many centuries the area was meadowland watered by the Tyburn, a stream which rose near Hampstead, flowed down across what is now Oxford Street and cut a curving way through what is now the Park to end as an irregular pool surrounded by marsh, roughly where the Victoria Memorial now stands in front of the Palace.

The meadows came into history in 1554 when forces supporting the Catholic Queen Mary made an armed camp there to stop that fine Englishman Sir Thomas Wyat and his Kentishmen, who had crossed the Thames at Kingston, from marching on London. The 'Green Park' forces cut off most of Wyat's men and defeated them in an engagement on Hay Hill, just north of what is Piccadilly. Wyat pressed on towards London, but to disastrous defeat and the block.

During the Civil War, a century later, Cromwellian troops fortified the area to seal off the western approaches to London. They used as barracks the nearby Goring House, built by the Royalist courtier, George (later Lord) Goring, the first of the mansions to be built on the site of Buckingham Palace.

In the Stuart Restoration of 1660 we have seen how expeditiously Charles II set to work to impose a classical French-style design on St James's Park. By 1668 the King decided it was time to organise 'Upper St James's Park', which is now Green Park. The rather sparse royal site was extended eastwards by 6

The Mall, looking west towards Buckingham Palace; St James's Park on the left, and Green Park, at the top of the Mall, on the right.

91

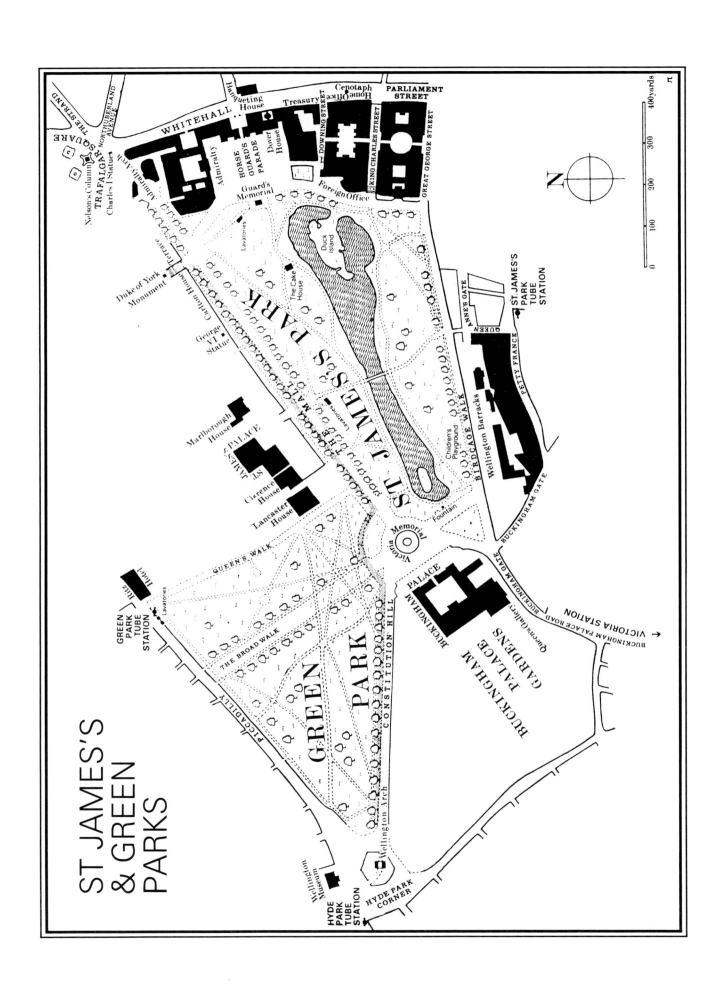

acres acquired from Sir William Pulteney* and, in time, added another 41 acres to the west, bought from the Davies Grosvenor Estate. The new Park was enclosed by a fine new wall, avenues of trees were planted, formal, gravelled paths were laid down and a herd of deer were introduced and segregated in a 'harbour', more or less where the Wellington Arch stands at the top of Constitution Hill.

A Ranger's Lodge was built for the official in charge and some work was done to improve the old track on the northern boundary which was now called the 'New Way to Kensington', the forerunner of the Piccadilly of today. There is an agreeable story that Constitution Hill owes its name to the King's habit of taking his constitutional from Whitehall, St James's Park and across what is now Green Park.

For Green Park, the 18th century was eventful. A canal or reservoir was excavated at the north-east end, roughly at what is now the entrance to Green Park underground station. This had to be enlarged in 1730 to enable the Chelsea Water Company to provide for the growing needs of St James's Palace, the Park, and Buckingham House. The reservoir was made more lively with a decorative fountain and became known as 'The Queen's Basin' at around the same time (1730) as 'The Queen's Walk' was being laid out along the eastern boundary. 'The Queen' was the redoubtable Caroline of Anspach, wife of George II. Her strong personality and her power over the Prime Minister, Sir Robert Walpole, led to many autocratic developments in the Royal Parks.

For example, the Queen's Walk was to be a private walk for herself and the royal family and at the Mall end she had built, to designs by William Kent, 'The Queen's Library'. This was in fact not much more than a summerhouse overlooking the Park, but its title reflected the sincere, if rather high-flown intellectual interests of the Queen.

This Library might have been the death of her, for one account says she caught cold walking there for breakfast on 9th November 1737. Other reports say that her fatal illness was caused by a rupture she had kept secret for years and that an operation was finally carried out, two days too late. She died in St James's Palace on the 20th of the month, aged 54.

On her death-bed she suggested to her husband that he should marry again. The King, not the most agreeable or attractive of men, seemed to have been moved by the scene and between sobs exclaimed: 'Non, j'aurai des maîtresses!' 'Ah, mon Dieu,' replied the Queen, 'cela n'empêche pas!' – as she knew only too well, for his stable of women had been part of her court for years.

* Later sold to Henry Bennet, Earl of Arlington, hence the modern 'Bennet Street' and 'Arlington Street'.

George, however, kept to his promises. He did not marry again and he did have mistresses.

In April, 1749, he witnessed from an ornate pavilion specially built near the Queen's Library the spectacular celebrations in the Park to commemorate the Peace of Aix-la-Chapelle which had been concluded the previous year.

The elaborate arrangements and the subsequent disaster epitomised the spuriousness of this 18th-century 'Age of Reason', including the senseless, destructive wars which engulfed Europe from 1740 to 1763, thus proving that the acclaimed 'Peace of Aix-la-Chapelle' was no more than a diplomatic sham. Fortunately, England was politically well led and only marginally involved in Europe,* and thus emerged vastly more rich and powerful from overseas trade and conquest.

So, perhaps, after all, England did have something to celebrate in Green Park!

For the King the day was very special. As Elector (ruler) of Hanover he was much more interested in the ebb and flow of affairs in Europe than most of his British subjects. In addition, in June 1743 he had been present at the victorious Battle of Dettingen against the French and thus became the last of our kings to have drawn his sword in armed conflict (though he was not to know this at the time).

In the morning he had reviewed three battalions of the Guards from a dais by the wall of St James's Palace. For him that was more a pleasure than a duty for it was said of him that he had the blinkered outlook of a drill-sergeant.

The preparations for the evening had been going on for many weeks at great expense but now all was ready. The firework display was eagerly anticipated as it promised to be the most lavish ever seen in England, if not in Europe, and would provide a spectacular background to the show-piece, an elaborate 'Temple of Peace' in the classical Greek Doric style, 114 ft high and 410 ft long. Handel had been commissioned to write music for a mainly military band of a hundred musicians which would nobly express martial glory. Its effect would be heightened by the intermittent firing of 100 cannon and the thrilling hissing and detonations of the massed fireworks ordered specially from Italy, among them 10,000 rockets, 12,000 fire sprays and 5,000 maroons. Handel's 'Music for the Royal Fireworks' did more than justice to the event.

Apart from the royal pavilion there were comfortable viewing galleries for the Privy Council, the House of Lords, the House of Commons, foreign diplomats and the dignitaries of the City of London, led by the Lord Mayor.

Beyond all these privileged enclosures there milled great crowds of people. All the Park gates had been opened and a long

* Mainly by providing subsidies which helped to keep the war going.

gap made in the wall facing Piccadilly to facilitate entrance.

Now came the great moment when the proceedings began. Royalty, the dignitaries and the commoners were in their places. The signal was given.

The martial music rolled and thundered with massed drums and trumpets; the fireworks began to dazzle the imagination and to illuminate the splendid scene; the cannon boomed regularly with dignity. Everything was going as planned. Exclamations of delight and wonder followed the rockets as they rose into the sky.

Then disaster struck. The roof of the Temple of Peace caught fire, perhaps from one of the falling rockets. With terrifying rapidity the entire area became engulfed in a series of fires and explosions as the thousands of fireworks, including huge set pieces, cascades and Catherine wheels, were prematurely set alight.

There was wild panic, not only among the unprotected crowds, but also in the privileged enclosures, for the galleries were flimsily built and ornately draped. Royalty was forced to retreat which was just as well, for the nearby Queen's Library caught fire and was badly damaged.

Many in the crowds were crushed and some died. Fortunately, St George's Hospital by Hyde Park Corner had just been opened and was able to provide swift help for the injured who were carried there.

The Temple of Peace had not lasted long, neither did the Treaty of Aix-la-Chapelle it celebrated.

Previous page: The fountain in Green Park in 1808. The eastern end of Green Park, around the Queen's Walk and the reservoir and fountain, became a fashionable resort during the latter part of the 18th century. Many fashionable people were by this time living in the new houses north of Piccadilly.

Below: The elaborate structure erected in Green Park for 'the Royal Fire Works Exhibited the 27th of April 1749 on account of the General Peace'. The 'Peace' was the Peace of Aix-la-Chapelle and Handel composed his Music for the Royal Fireworks for this same occasion. Unfortunately it ended in disaster. The roof of the Temple of Peace, shown here, caught fire and thousands of fireworks were prematurely set alight. In the ensuing panic, many were hurt, some fatally.

George II was succeeded on his death in 1760 by his grand-son, George III, since Frederick, Prince of Wales had died in 1751. In 1761 the new King, who was 23, married the 17-year-old Charlotte of Mecklenburg-Strelitz in the chapel of St James's Palace. The following year, 1762, the King bought Buckingham House, on which the royal family had long had its eye. At first it was intended as the young Queen's Dower House and was known as 'The Queen's House', but George III was a family man and made it his London home and there Charlotte bore him fourteen children (the eldest, the future Prince Regent and George IV was born at St James's Palace).

The purchase of Buckingham House was not good for Green Park. George III decided to extend the royal gardens and took over an extensive slice of the Park which lay to the west of what is now Constitution Hill.

Nevertheless, the eastern end of Green Park, around the Queen's Walk and the reservoir and fountain, became a fashionable resort during the latter part of the century, partly because St James's Park was deteriorating physically and socially and partly because many fashionable people were now living in the new houses north of Piccadilly. The scene during the hours of promenade around the Queen's Walk must have been very colourful and agreeable, for during the Regency period there was an elegance of dress and manners such as has rarely been seen in England.

Inevitably, as it became fashionable, the Park took over from St James's as the scene of dawn duels, those ridiculous confrontations which sometimes cost valuable lives to satisfy so-called honour, said to be damaged in what was more often than not a drunken quarrel.

The Napoleonic Wars, which for so many years had impoverished Europe and tested Britain's will to the uttermost, seemed to have come to an end in the spring of 1814 when the French Emperor was forced to abdicate as Russian, German and British armies occupied France.

With Napoleon apparently safely banished to Elba, a generous peace was concluded with France where the Bourbon Louis XVIII now reigned after his years of exile in England.

It was a suitable time for national rejoicing and Green Park was chosen as one of the principal sites. The beginning of August 1814 marked the centenary of the accession of the House of Hanover in England, so it was decided to combine the two celebrations, even though the Prince Regent* was now so unpopular in London that the streets had often to be cleared before he drove out from his palace, Carlton House.

---

* The mental health of George III had deteriorated so badly by 1811 that the Prince of Wales had been created Prince Regent. He became King George IV when his father died in 1820.

Nearly a third of the Park from Constitution Hill downwards was taken over and an imaginative design for the temporary buildings was produced by Sir William Congreve. As in 1749 they were to be the background for a huge firework display.

There was a great medieval castle with round tower and ramparts in the 'Gothick' style made fashionable first by Horace Walpole in *The Castle of Otranto* and then popularised by such 'terror' novelists as Mrs Radcliffe and 'Monk' Lewis.

So the mock castle, impressive in itself, also had a special appeal to the literati. But there was another aspect which interested the forward-looking, mechanical men, or technologists as we would call them today.

The entire structure slowly revolved so that the spectators could view all the scenes painted on the castle walls which recalled the great heroes and triumphs of the British people, culminating in the victory over Napoleon.

This was Stage One of the celebrations which were to be illuminated by a massed display of fireworks, including batteries of rockets, and punctuated by the roar of cannon.

As with the Peace of Aix-la-Chapelle display, stands had been erected for privileged spectators and a temporary bridge had been constructed from the garden wall of St James's Palace to enable the Prince Regent and his guests to reach their viewing gallery in comfort.

On the same evening there were elaborate celebrations designed by Nash in St James's Park, including a Rialto-style bridge across the canal surmounted with a Chinese pagoda and another firework display. As described in the chapter on St James's Park, the pagoda caught fire, much of the burning débris fall into the canal; several workmen were killed, others injured.

The crowds in and around Green Park were soon aware of this tremendous blaze a few hundred yards away and decided it promised livelier entertainment than a slowly revolving castle with historical scenes they could hardly see or understand. Rumours quickly spread of deaths and injuries, giving an added impetus to the exodus to St James's Park.

The privileged spectators watched developments with growing unease. They saw the crowds surging towards St James's Park to view the pagoda in flames. Their interest began to wane in the Gothick castle.

Then word went round that the Prince Regent and his party were not coming. It seems that he had, naturally enough, invited a large number of guests to a reception in Carlton House which overlooked St James's Park. When the pagoda caught fire and the excited yells and screams of the crowd penetrated the salons of Carlton House, the Prince Regent was advised that his appearance in Green Park to watch the celebrations there might provoke public disorder and personal danger to himself.

Victoria and Albert were shot at again from Green Park in 1842. On Sunday evening, 29th May, when they returned to the Palace from their drive Albert told her that he thought he had seen a man trying to aim a pistol at them. Later they received information that an armed man had indeed been seen lurking in the neighbourhood.

The next day, Monday, Victoria ordered the carriage for her usual drive with Albert and would listen to no protests. In fact, they went without guards and left behind the lady-in-waiting who would normally have been in attendance. Victoria seems to have decided to try and provoke the man to use his pistol.

The drive proved uneventful at first and they were coming down Constitution Hill by the Palace when a small, swarthy man darted forward to the railings of Green Park. Albert recognised him, but could do nothing before the man fired. A policeman seized him immediately. Victoria stood up in the carriage, with Albert at her side, to show they were unharmed.

This time the assailant, Francis, was sentenced to death, but the Queen asked for this to be changed to transportation for life.

Two attempts on Victoria's life from Green Park might be considered more than enough, but there was a third incident on 19th May 1849 and although the gun proved to be unloaded, Victoria was not to know that when the man aimed the weapon at her, cocked it and pulled the trigger.

Victoria was driving up Constitution Hill with her three eldest children, Vicki, Bertie (the future Edward VII) and Alice. Albert was riding ahead on his own.

The man with the pistol was immediately seized by several passers-by. Victoria once again stood up calmly to show she was unhurt. The children looked bewildered as Albert galloped back to the carriage.

The assailant was an Irishman, Hamilton by name, who was found to be mentally unstable. The fact that he was an Irishman, however, was at that time chilling. After the Irish potato famines of 1845–6 when thousands died and even more emigrated mainly to America, the spirit of revolt led by the Fenians, predecessors of the IRA, rose in the island. In 1848 there was armed rebellion, bloodily subdued, leaving a legacy of simmering hatred.

To all appearances serenely immune from these violent dramas, the Green Park went on in its quiet way, changing with the seasons in decorous fashion. In the first decade of this century the Broad Walk was given a more formal appearance as part of a vista from Piccadilly down through the Park to the ornamental gates presented by the then Dominion of Canada. These led to the gardens round the massive statue of Queen Victoria in front of Buckingham Palace unveiled by George V in 1911. The northern end of the vista was greatly enriched in 1921 when the magnificent iron gates which had stood guard

Following page: The magnificently elaborate Canada Gates, at the Victoria Memorial entrance to Green Park.

105

over Devonshire House on the north side of Piccadilly were bought from the then Duke of Devonshire who had sold the family town-house for redevelopment.

It cannot be said that there has been much other good news about the Green Park. The Horse Ride has been kept in good order by the side of the Constitution Hill thoroughfare. Spring bulbs are planted along the Piccadilly boundary as plentifully as the budget allows. Ground has been lost at the top of Constitution Hill to make room for a traffic roundabout, but attempts have been made to 'landscape', as they say, the bleak ugliness with grass and flower-beds.

The old bandstand near the Queen's Walk where in a circle of plane trees military bands had played for public pleasure was neglected for so many years that it became derelict and was demolished in 1980.

By far the worst desecration the Green Park has suffered since the war has, unfortunately, been unavoidable. As the development of London's Underground system proceeded first with the Victoria, then the Jubilee Lines, Green Park Station became an essential link in the massive operation. A large section of the Park in this area had to be appropriated and was a busy contractors' yard for years. It was, inevitably, an eyesore and it has taken time and money to bring the area back to its former self.

As for the future of the Green Park, the financial stringency imposed on budgets by central government in recent years precludes almost any plans for improvements in any of the Royal Parks, but hopefully there will come a day when circumstances will be more favourable. Although I and many others would be glad to see the Park transformed with terraces and fountains, there would be opponents to any change in the Park's present character. They enthuse over the presence in central London of a tranquil landscape of trees and grass where office workers can picnic at lunch-time and travellers in traffic jams can be transported momentarily to a country scene.

There might well be opposition to change from a very influential quarter. In my research for a book on Buckingham Palace I became aware that the private apartments of the Queen and Prince Philip are on the first floor of the north wing which overlooks Green Park. Below the windows are flower-beds of great beauty along the base of the high wall of the Palace which hides the traffic of Constitution Hill. Beyond are the trees and grass of Green Park, evoking the countryside and effectively deadening the noise of the traffic along Piccadilly. Thus the present lay-out of Green Park extends the tranquillity of the Palace beyond its walls. It might be thought that major changes would disturb this peace.

107

Regent's Park and Primrose Hill

NASH INTENDED CUMBERLAND TERRACE, stretching 800 ft along the east side of the Outer Circle of Regent's Park, to be the overwhelming coup de théâtre of the entire development: Regent's Park was not only his greatest achievement but also cast reflected glory on his patrons, including the Prince Regent and a group of enlightened officials. They gave him the opportunity, here and elsewhere, to transform parts of central London from the shambles of uncoordinated growth into the framework of a capital city worthy of a country emerging from the Napoleonic Wars as the most powerful in the world.

Cumberland Terrace was nobly inspired by the classical style which had long dominated English taste in an educated class, disciplined in Greek and Latin during youth, and then launched on a leisurely Grand Tour during which the beauties of antiquity shared attention with those of the present.

Nash's Regent's Park is a superb memorial to that Augustan period of English taste, already by that time assailed by the Gothic Revival. What is even more superb is that it is still a living part of the London scene.

Regent's Park, like St James's, Hyde Park and Kensington Gardens, was originally monastic farmland taken over by Henry VIII and turned into a hunting preserve. The King's greed has, in the long run, benefited the people though I doubt if that Tudor monster would have approved!

The Regent's Park area, then known as Marylebone Park, was sold off during the Commonwealth period to three cavalry officers in Cromwell's Army who cut down most of the trees for there was a ready market, especially for the oaks, as their timber was urgently needed to build warships. The herds of deer were sold, like those of Hyde Park, to landowners and butchers.

At the Restoration Charles II took back the land but did not compensate the temporary owners as he had those who had bought Hyde Park under the Commonwealth. The estate was, however, let to others as farmland. As London grew there was a

West Gate, Regent's Park, also known as Hanover Gate, still survives today.

109

good livelihood providing dairy produce from herds of cows, and hay from the meadows for the thousands of horses in the capital.

By the 18th century the main leases were held by the Dukes of Portland, descendants of Bentinck, the lifelong friend of William of Orange, who lavished lands and titles on him when he became King of England.

These leases were due to expire in 1811 and a remarkably imaginative official, John Fordyce, Surveyor-General of His Majesty's Land Revenue, obtained approval in 1793 for the offer of £1,000 to the architect who produced the most suitable comprehensive development plan for the area. No schemes at all, however, had been submitted by the time Fordyce died in 1809. His office was then combined with the Office of Woods and Forests in which Nash had three years earlier been appointed architect to the Chief Commissioner, in all likelihood due to the influence of the Prince Regent.

Nash enjoyed the favour of the Prince Regent, but it is a matter of debate whether he owed that favour initially to his talents or to his marriage with Mary Anne Bradley in December 1798 when he was 46 and she, 25. Probably she had been the Prince Regent's mistress and the five children she brought up as relatives, under the name of Pennethorne, were his offspring. Certainly Nash, who had been no more than prosperous before his marriage, began then to live as a very rich man. He designed and built for himself an impressive town house in Dover Street, Mayfair, and a country house, East Cowes Castle, on the Isle of Wight where he bought a large estate. His purse always seemed to be full and he entertained on a noble scale.

All this prosperity made life easy for Nash, in spite of outspoken gossip and ribald lampoons. More important for posterity, however, were the unique architectural opportunities which unfolded for him, thanks to the patronage of the Prince Regent. That old cynic Voltaire would have relished the story of the English architect who only got the chance to show his genius after wisely marrying the discarded, but well-endowed mistress of royalty.

When the leases of Marylebone Park were about to fall in, two development plans were produced. Nash's was daring and imaginative, the other pedestrian and dull. Behind the scenes the Prince Regent exerted his influence, for by this time he realised that in Nash he had found the man who instinctively understood his grandiose architectural ambitions and could realise them. The Marylebone Park plan was accepted by the Treasury with modifications which reduced the number of buildings in order to preserve more parkland.

At the same time, however, Nash was working on the idea which had been put forward by Fordyce for a splendid new thoroughfare which would link Charing Cross to the new

111

estates of Marylebone Park, thus enabling members of Parliament and other men of influence and wealth in and around Whitehall to make the journey with speed and comfort.

Previous page: Roses in Queen Mary's Garden, Regent's Park.

Nash made it come true, with the help of the Prince Regent and the benign assistance of the Treasury which saw great profit from the development of an area, largely Crown property, which by now had passed to the State in return for royal annuities and grants. It was an extraordinary achievement and we can still follow Nash's thoroughfare today. Starting from St James's Park, the route takes us up Lower Regent Street to Piccadilly Circus and then turning left continues up Regent Street, past Oxford Circus and Portland Place into Regent's Park.

For the Prince Regent himself the new route was to be a 'Via Triumphalis' from his palace, Carlton House, overlooking St James's Park, to a countrified villa or pleasure pavilion, ('guingette' was the fashionable term used) to be built in Regent's Park facing the Ionic columns, noble pediments and gesticulating statues of Cumberland Terrace. It was not to be. Carlton House was pulled down. The 'guingette' was never built.

The Prince Regent may not have had any martial triumphs to celebrate along the 'Via', but the creation of Regent Street and Regent's Park, in which he played so large a part, commemorates a triumph of a kind rare in this country, a triumph of taste. It is good that he is remembered in their name, unworthy as he was in so many other ways.

Having said that, it should be pointed out that Regent Street and Regent's Park were designed for the nobility and the rich, with the lower orders who provided them with the necessary services kept in their place.

Nash was praised for the bold sweep of Regent Street between Piccadilly Circus and Oxford Circus, for it would act as a barrier between the often foreign workers of Soho in the east and the upper classes living in Mayfair to the west.

To a certain extent it did have this effect for a short time, but the daily business of life in a great city made it impossible to shut off one area from another. Each needed the other. In addition, Londoners of all classes would have soon been bored by a half-empty Via Triumphalis. Regent Street has survived by changing with the times.

Regent's Park is another matter. The fantasy world still exists in much the same form as when Nash designed it.

For it is a fantasy world rising almost dream-like in the centre of London, a few yards from the Marylebone Road with its offices, shops and relentless flow of traffic.

It is as if Nash created for the Prince Regent a stage design from which all the ugliness of life has been magically banished. No hovels, no ragged poor, no sick and old – they have no part in such a world.

112

the meantime deteriorated. The Marquess, who had been fascinated by the clock as a boy, was with his influence able to buy it and had it placed on the facade of his new Regent's Park villa. It seems strange that a man like Hertford could ever have been a boy who took pleasure in such simple form!

Much later St Dunstan's Villa acquired real nobility. It was used during and after the First World War to rehabilitate and train thousands of servicemen blinded, often by poison gas. After the villa was vacated this fine work was still carried on by the St Dunstan's Association.

In the 1930s the first Lord Rothermere leased the villa. He had inherited the great press empire created by his elder brother, Lord Northcliffe, the virtual creator of modern journalism. Rothermere, like the 3rd Marquess of Hertford, was a man of pleasure as well as of business and enjoyed relaxing and entertaining his friends there. As a newspaper proprietor in Fleet Street, however, he had some qualms about the St Dunstan's clock and in a mood of piety arranged for it to be restored to its original position over the church in Fleet Street.

It was almost inevitable to complete the circle that Mrs Maria Fitzherbert, a Roman Catholic, whom the Prince Regent had illegally married in December 1785, should have lived for a time in one of the villas in Regent's Park. She was 29, quite beautiful and had already been widowed twice when the Prince Regent, six years younger, went through the marriage ceremony both knew would never be recognised, in order to satisfy her conscience and her Church, which it seems to have done in both cases.

They had many happy years together, interrupted for a time when he made his unfortunate marriage to Caroline of Brunswick-Wolfenbüttel. Even when the Prince Regent brought the relationship to a cruelly abrupt end he provided for her handsomely enough, although there were no children. She outlived him by seven years.

It is pleasant to record that she was treated with courtesy by the Prince's parents, George III and Queen Charlotte, and with kindness by his brother, William IV and his wife, Queen Adelaide. She was also for years on intimate terms with the men and women of the Hertford family. It was a closely-knit circle!

I mentioned that 'The Holme' had until recently been occupied by Bedford College before it moved to Egham. The main buildings of the College, which have also been vacated, are an undistinguished block a few hundred yards to the south. They are on the site of South Villa (built 1827) which was demolished to make room for the new development.

The College had been founded in Bloomsbury at Bedford Square as early as 1849 and has thus achieved distinction as the oldest institution in the country for the higher education of women.

When the plans for the new buildings were announced around 1910 there were angry protests from near and far. The arguments were varied, but centred on the fact that one of the original villas was being destroyed to make way for a college which would educate 'The New Woman', that frightening being described by Ibsen and Shaw, and widely considered a phenomenon more threatening to the established order than anarchists or revolutionaries.

The tide, however, was flowing strongly in favour of woman's emancipation and Queen Mary, outwardly conservative, but in fact a great supporter of women's rights, was delighted to open the new College buildings in 1913 at a time when the Suffragette Movement was battling, sometimes violently, for Votes for Women.

In time the College was able to lease the attractive St John's Lodge, the first of the villas to be built in the Park, to serve as a residence for senior members of the staff. It lies on the northern side of the Inner Circle and was designed in graceful classical style by John Raffield. Perhaps its most illustrious tenant has been the elder brother of Wellington, the Marquess of Wellesley, who won fame and fortune as a soldier and administrator in India.

The gardens, now open to the public, are an enchantment. High clipped hedges enclose a magic world of flower-beds, lawns, statues and splashing waters.

The future of the Bedford College site which altogether covers ten acres was in doubt for much of 1983 and 1984. One of the conditions of the Crown Commissioners' lease, which has 25 years to run, was that the buildings could be used only for educational purposes. At first an Arab group was interested, but finally a consortium of American university institutions, headed by Rockford College of Illinois, won the day. In August 1984 it was announced that the consortium will pay an annual rent of £800,000 for seven years, with five-yearly reviews. More than £4m will be spent on refurbishing to which the Crown Commissioners will contribute £1,750,000.

There was resentment, even a sense of humiliation that this magnificent site, unique in its urban situation, had been lost to British education. There had been hopes that perhaps the Central London Polytechnic or a combination of St Martin's School of Art and the London College of Fashion might have had a chance of moving there. Unfortunately, the Inner London Education Authority was forced to the decision that in the prevailing monetarist climate there was no possibility of finding the money necessary.

It is, however, no use repining, especially as the Americans have been such munificent benefactors of our ancient seats of learning. Students of Rockford and 14 associated American universities will have the opportunity of spending six months of

119

their degree course studying cultural and liberal arts in London. If they are at all receptive to atmosphere what better environment could they have than Regent's Park for such studies? A good augury for the future is that the site has been named Regent's College.

Previous page: The lake in Queen Mary's Garden.

With Winfield House, the residence of the US Ambassador, also in its boundaries, Regent's Park will soon acquire, like Grosvenor Square, dominated by the US Embassy, a strong American flavour.

In Nash's original plan the Inner Circle of the Park was to have been ringed with houses in their own gardens which would have turned the area into a private enclave. Although the scheme would have increased the income of the Crown Estate it was fortunately shelved and in time the area has acquired a distinct personality, open to public enjoyment.

It has always been a favoured haunt of Flora in her most elaborate urban costume. Soon after Queen Victoria came to the throne in 1837 the Royal Botanical Society leased 18 acres and commissioned Decimus Burton to lay out the gardens and design the buildings. How lucky that he was available! Throughout the Victorian era and well into this century the gardens flourished and the annual flower show was part of the London Season. Unfortunately for the Society the lease came up for renewal in 1932 and the Crown Commissioners demanded a rent that was quite impossible.

When the Royal Parks Department, then attached to the Ministry of Works, took the grounds over, they were renamed Queen Mary's Gardens in honour of the wife of the reigning monarch, George V. Under the new management it was decided to make one area a rose-garden of such splendour that it would soon become world-famous. So it turned out. The rose-garden, which is now almost universally called 'Queen Mary's Rose-Garden', has become in the summer months an attraction for tens of thousands of visitors from home and abroad. There are said to be 30,000 rose-bushes in 100 beds which produce an overwhelming display reminiscent of the Victorian and Edwardian 'carpet-bedding' which was more often an expression of wealth than of taste.

As well as the massed roses, other delights within a few steps include the small ornamental lake, frequented by water-fowl, and a waterfall refreshing to the spirit. There is even a miniature island you can reach over a high-arched bridge to admire the rockery plants and alpines. It is no wonder that the staff are confident this is far and away the best garden in the whole of the Royal Parks.

Not far from the roses and the lake is a pleasant restaurant built in recent years. The architects have given it a tapering pyramid-shape roof reminiscent of Decimus Burton's design for 'The Tent Room' of St Dunstan's Villa. The same archi-

120

tectural conceit can be seen in two other post-war Royal Parks buildings – The Cake House in St James's Park and the Serpentine Restaurant in Hyde Park.

Another agreeable feature of the Inner Circle is a mound which rises gently not far from the waterfall. It is modest compared with the imposing mount raised in Kensington Gardens during the 18th century as part of the improvements carried out by Bridgman for Queen Caroline. That mount, however, was later levelled, but this mound survives. It was formed from the earth excavated to make the large lake in the Park, just as the material for the Kensington Gardens mount came from digging out the Long Water and the Serpentine.

Nearby in the Inner Circle is a very attractive fountain which rises from as seductive a group of mermaids as ever tempted a seafarer. The sculptor was William McMillan and it was accepted as a gift from the Constance Foundation in 1950. The site, set among lake and gardens, seems just right and around its base tulips and roses flower in season.

John Nash's plan of the improvements to Regent's Park, dated 1839.

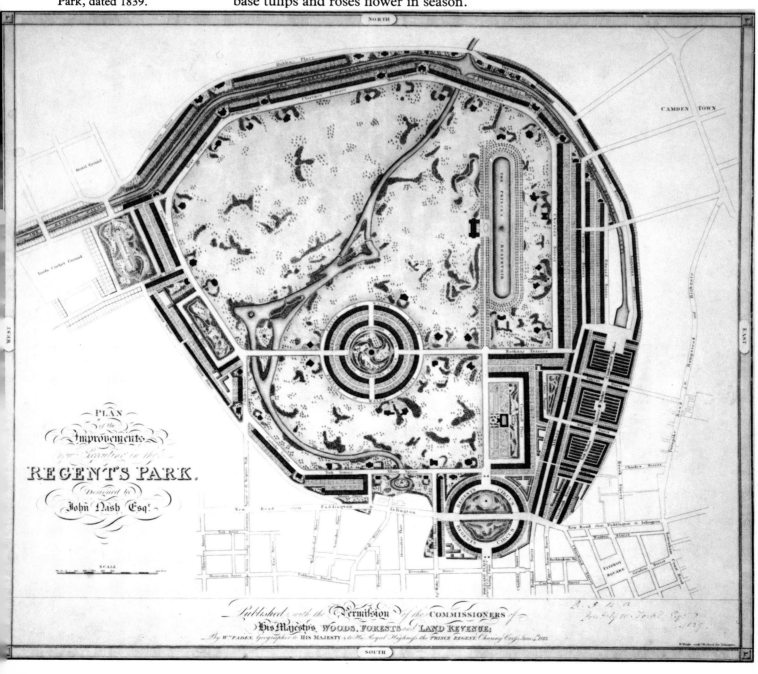

The Royal Parks are now chary of accepting new sculptures or memorials. In Victorian and Edwardian days too many were put up and now tend to litter the Parks, for example the rather pathetic headstones in the long-closed cemetery for dogs, cats and cage-birds which lies near the Victoria Gate of Hyde Park by the Bayswater Road.

It is right that those who gave their lives in the two World Wars should be nobly remembered in and around such public places as the Royal Parks, but otherwise I agree with the authorities that enough is enough.*

The Inner Circle is also the home of the Open Air Theatre, a remarkable venture started in 1932 by that imaginative director Sidney Carroll, and now flourishing under David Conville who has been in charge since 1962.

Coiling around the Inner Circle is the main lake of the Park covering 22 acres. It is as beguiling an exercise in creative landscaping as the genius of Nash ever conceived. When it was completed in the early 1820s discerning observers were enthusiastic and it became one of the favoured sights of London, but in this second half of the 20th century I would not say it has received the recognition it deserves.

The old magician (for Nash was then in his sixties) had waved his wand over Marylebone Park and out of marshy ground around the course of the Tyburn stream had conjured what seems a confluence of broad rivers flowing majestically to some distant sea, against a background of splendid white-shining palaces surrounded by rich parkland gently rising to northern hills.

You could call it a trick, I suppose. But then landscaping is, inevitably, something of a trick, manipulating nature to an artificial design. In his instinctive, somewhat predatory way Nash had acquired much of his landscaping skill from Humphry Repton, a man of poetic, imaginative talent who had taken on the mantle of the great 'Capability' Brown. Nash and Repton, who also had architectural talents, were for a time in partnership, but Nash with his royal patronage later overshadowed poor Repton. His plans for the Royal Pavilion at Brighton were taken out of his hands and finally developed by Nash. It is not surprising that Repton joined the growing ranks of Nash's enemies.

When you look at the map of Regent's Park it is quite easy to visualise Nash's original plan if you realise that the lake would have been fringed with villas in extensive grounds like The Holme, and that the waters would undoubtedly have reached the grounds of the Prince Regent's intended guingette. When

Previous pages: Two views of Regent's Park.

* An exception has been made, however, in Kensington Gardens where an abstract sculpture of 1979, a gift from the Henry Moore Foundation, has been placed near the Long Water.

124

terrible illness, the Prince Regent had knighted him at the age of 35, so there was a link already between Raffles and Regent's Park when he obtained the lease for the Zoo.

Fortunately, Decimus Burton was available as architect and designed in his elegant style the first buildings, cages and aviaries.* The Royal Menagerie long installed at the Tower of London was transferred to Regent's Park, other private collections followed and were soon augmented by gifts and purchases from many parts of the world.

It was not long before the collection at the London Zoo became world-famous. This was an epoch when the all-powerful, self-confident British got results -- quickly.

Motives were, as is usual, mixed. Serious-minded men such as Raffles, Davy and other Fellows of the Zoological Society wanted to spread useful knowledge about a world which was being rapidly opened up, often by the British.

For many, however, the Zoo became a distraction, amusing on the surface, but also disturbingly exciting as the lions, tigers and other predators gazed menacingly from their cages at the spectators.

There was, however, a really jolly occasion at the Zoo on Friday 8th June 1984 when Mrs Nancy Reagan entertained there a group of 40 deprived London children between the ages of 4 and 14. She was staying at Winfield House, in Regent's Park, with her husband, the President of the USA, who was attending the Western summit meetings. Whilst he was at the various talks, Mrs Reagan had little freedom to move around for security was adamantine. She managed to visit the Princess of Wales and her first-born, Prince William, at Kensington Palace, but her only public engagement during her visit was just along the road from Winfield House, at the Zoo. That highly benevolent organisation, the Variety Club of Great Britain, had organised everything for the children, from a ride in a London double-decker bus to a picnic lunch of ham sandwiches, chicken legs, jelly and cake washed down with orange juice and Coke. A two-week-old reindeer was named 'Nancy' in Mrs Reagan's honour; she fed a four-year-old Sri Lankan elephant. Even allowing for the public relations aspect she looked as if she was really enjoying herself.

Not surprising! She had escaped for a few hours and was talking to real people, who were not involved in politics.

In 1984 the Zoo helped to bring back the native red squirrel to Regent's Park for the first time in 50 years – a remarkable turn of fortune.

It has long been part of accepted lore that the larger American grey squirrel had years ago killed or driven away the reds in

* In post-war years the Earl of Snowdon has designed a large new aviary of wire mesh which has an agreeable lightness of touch appropriate to its subject.

most of Britain. Now, the experts think the explanation is that the greys were more adaptable than the reds in surviving periods of food shortage.

In Scotland the reds have continued to flourish because there are coniferous forests to provide a plentiful source of food. In Fife they have been breeding so plentifully that they have become a pest in some areas, and from here a few pairs have been brought down to the Zoo to be conditioned to an urban environment before being let loose in the Park. There they will be helped by special food hoppers and nest boxes scattered around a wide area, and they will also have access back to their Zoo homes in case they find freedom too precarious.

'It could be,' said a Zoo official, 'that the squirrels depart by the next train to Scotland, or disappear into the bowels of Kilburn' (a not-too-distant district with a strong Irish accent). 'We just hope they stay.'

So do we all. An encouraging thought is Dr Johnson's judgment that 'the noblest prospect which a Scotchman ever sees is the high road that leads him to England'.

Beyond the Zoo, the canal and Prince Albert Road lies Primrose Hill, an open space of 120 acres, which is administratively part of Regent's Park. It was acquired from Eton College in 1842 in return for land at Windsor, with the well-meaning intention of providing a splendid view of central London from the summit of the 200 ft high hill.

The view is fine indeed, but, sadly, two panoramas identifying the many notable landmarks have each in turn been destroyed by vandals. Unfortunately, Primrose Hill, never known for its primroses, has a history of violence. Sir Edmund Berry Godfrey, a magistrate who had taken evidence from Titus Oates, the Popish Plot villain, was found in a ditch there spiked on his own sword with his purse untouched. Other deaths resulted not so much from duelling as bloody affrays. There are still problems today – muggings and senseless destruction – so that, for example, it has proved useless to plant flower-beds there.

Probably the most agreeable scenes on Primrose Hill take place when there is a good fall of snow that freezes. Then the toboggans are brought out and the crisp air is full of the shouts and laughter of the children – and the adults – as they career down the slopes. Nowadays skiers are also quick to take the opportunity to practise, and soon make a *piste* of sorts.

Such happy scenes dispel even the baleful words of Mother Shipton, 'the wise woman' of Yorkshire, who prophesied in the 18th century, 'When London surrounds Primrose Hill the streets of the Metropolis will run with blood.'

In the south-west of Regent's Park beyond Hanover Terrace

130

the minaret and dome of the Central Mosque of London rise from the cool arcades of the Islamic Cultural Centre alongside. The impressive complex, built in classically elegant Moslem style, was completed in 1972 when the Arab world was beginning to become rich from oil revenues. Islam had, however, been established in this area of the Park some years earlier. Lady Ribblesdale, American by birth, had helped to finance the first Islamic Centre. The British government, mindful of residual imperial responsibilities, also helped. As it turned out, this was a wise move for the Moslem population of Britain has multiplied and so has the wealth and world-power of the Middle East oil states.

Previous page: The Boating Lake in Regent's Park.

At No. 10 in nearby Hanover Terrace lived one of our finest composers, Vaughan Williams, and at No. 13 lived and died the writer H. G. Wells.

The most intriguing tenant of the terrace in this century, however, was surely Mrs Wallis Simpson, who lived for a time in No. 7 when she had left her husband in 1936 preparatory to divorce. She got the divorce (her second) easily enough but the new King, Edward VIII, who had fallen in love with her years previously when he was Prince of Wales, was soon made to realise by the British Establishment that he would never be permitted to make her the first American Queen of England. To marry her he abdicated on 10th December 1936, and they lived for many years as Duke and Duchess of Windsor.

For Regent's Park the episode has all the ingredients of a drama of the absurd. No doubt with discreet royal help, Wallis Simpson was given a lease by the Crown Commissioners on a house in Hanover Terrace. Hanover, indeed, the original home of the dynasty from which Edward VIII was descended!

At this time of supreme crisis in her life, she might have looked out on Regent's Park in the direction of the villa of Mrs Fitzherbert, the Roman Catholic, who had undoubtedly been married to the Prince Regent and who had shared many happy years with him.

So the groves of Regent's Park can claim to have sheltered two women who would have both been Queen of England if it had not been for political and social taboos which stopped George IV and Edward VIII from having their way.

The war of 1939–45 took a terrible toll of Regent's Park. Holford House, which many consider to have been the finest of the villas built by Decimus Burton, was completely destroyed by bombs. Many other houses suffered severe damage. Repairs were minimal and as the dreary war years went on Nash's great terraces began to crumble and decay.

There were, however, enlightened men in the Labour government which came to power in 1945, and the Prime Minister, Mr (later Earl) Attlee, was devoted to London. The Crown Commissioners got down to the enormous task of restor-

132

ation, which often turned into reconstruction for, as has been mentioned, much of the original work had been shoddy.

It has taken a very long time indeed and cost a great deal of money, but now, over forty years after the end of the war, the work is just about complete and one of the finest urban architectural set pieces in the world rises with splendour among well-tended parkland to the delight and, perhaps, astonishment, of all.

It is appropriate that this, the finest memorial to the genius of Nash and the taste and imagination of his royal patron, should be in – Regent's Park.

Kew Gardens

KEW GREEN EXTENDS in a pleasing semicircle round the main entrance to the Gardens. In the middle of the green is the modest semiroyal church of St Anne where Queen Mary's grandfather, Prince Adolphus Frederick, Duke of Cambridge, the seventh son of King George III, lies in a mausoleum alongside her grandmother, the Princess Augusta of Hesse-Cassel, who was a great-granddaughter of King George II.

Those forbears of Queen Mary sum up the history of Kew Gardens: George II and his Queen, Caroline of Anspach; their son, Frederick, Prince of Wales (who did not live to succeed) and his wife, Augusta of Saxe-Coburg-Altenburg; and their son, George III, who married Charlotte of Mecklenburg-Strelitz.

George II bought the Richmond Lodge estate which ran along the river from Richmond Green towards Kew in 1721 when he was Prince of Wales. He and his wife, Caroline, wanted to have a home for themselves near London away from George I who heartily detested both of them. It was on the 14th June 1727 that the Prime Minister, Sir Robert Walpole, rode hard to Richmond, and made Caroline waken her husband from his after-dinner sleep to tell him his father had died on a visit to Hanover and that he was now King.

It was not until 1730 that Prince Frederick, the eldest son of George II and Caroline, bought the White House estate which adjoined the Richmond Lodge property and extended to Kew Green, as the Gardens do today. Frederick and Augusta also needed a haven, for in the continuing wretched Hanoverian tradition they were hated by George II and Caroline, who had now largely deserted Richmond Lodge for Hampton Court.

Both estates had once formed part of the great royal domain, formerly called Sheen, whose name the first Tudor monarch, Henry VII, changed to Richmond, the Yorkshire earldom he had held before he won the crown in 1485 on Bosworth Field from Richard III.

These royal lands were, however, sold off under the

Opposite: The famous Cedar Vista with the Chinese Pagoda at the far end.

135

Commonwealth in the 17th century, after the defeat and execution of Charles I. I have already described how this happened to some of the Royal Parks in Central London and how they were restored to the Crown when Charles II returned in 1660. But these properties between Richmond and Kew were left in private hands and had to be purchased back by the Hanoverians.

It is from those two estates that Kew Gardens, as we know them now, were formed.

We have already seen how that innovative landscape gardener, Charles Bridgman, virtually created Kensington Gardens for Queen Caroline so it was to be expected that she should commission him to make improvements on the Richmond Lodge estate. His romantic ornamental buildings, the 'Hermitage' and 'Merlin's Cave', which created quite a stir at the time, have long since disappeared.

Prince Frederick and his wife, Augusta, however, proved more significant in the history of the Gardens. Closely linked with both of them in the story is John Stuart, third Earl of Bute, who owed his friendship with Frederick to happening to be around to make up a game of whist during a downpour of rain at the Egham races. Bute possessed many of the necessary qualities of a courtier. He was handsome, ingratiating, quite able and with wide interests, which included botany.

At Richmond he swiftly became a favourite with Frederick and Augusta, preoccupied as they were at that time with producing children (in all, eight).

Frederick employed William Kent, whose summerhouses for Caroline in Kensington Gardens have already been noticed, to improve the White House and the gardens which had long been famous for their fruit. The Prince was soon induced by Bute to import plants, then rare, from abroad and began to form an exciting garden of exotics near the White House.

The unfortunate Frederick did not have long to cultivate his

Below: The gates to the Royal Botanical Gardens at Kew.

Opposite: William Chambers' drawing of the Chinese Pagoda.

The Great Pagoda

gardens for he died of complications following a chill in 1751 at the age of 44, leaving Augusta the task of bringing up the children, including the eldest son, George, now Prince of Wales. She took it all in her stride for she was a strong-minded and capable woman.

Bute was soon established as Augusta's intimate confidant as well as tutor to George. Then stories began to circulate, first in court circles and then beyond, that he was consoling the widow. The rumours may well have been true and it is likely that the forceful Augusta would have been the wooer. As Bute's political power grew so did the hatred of the mob for him. There were frequent riots enlivened by bonfires of a jackboot and petticoat, symbolising Bute and Augusta.

So far as the future of Kew Gardens was concerned, however, Bute's influence over Augusta proved most beneficial. He introduced her to the architect, Sir William Chambers, whose work in the 1760s still adorns the Gardens. The elegant Orangery near the main gates is much admired as are his three graceful 'temples' which have survived – Bellona, Aeolus and Arethusa. The most attractive is the Temple of Aeolus whose delicate columns crown the artificial mound beyond the lake in front of the Palm House. Chambers was fortunate for when it fell into decay it was rebuilt in 1845 by Decimus Burton.

During that Augustan age in England it was fashionable not only to embellish estates with classical temples, but also to have a reproduction of a classical ruin which would recall the Italian landscape so much admired by English people making the Grand Tour. So Chambers designed for Kew a Roman triumphal arch, in appearance worn by time and vandalised by barbarians, and you can walk through it now admiring the picturesque way in which dilapidated masonry and sculpture lie nearby in carefully contrived abandon.

Chambers was also given the opportunity at Kew of displaying the architectural fruits of his travels which had extended as far as China. His Pagoda still rises ten storeys high in the southeast corner of the Gardens. I had always thought it looked solitary and somewhat out of place, but later I learned Chambers had flanked it with a Moorish Alhambra and an Arabic mosque, both of which were later demolished. The three buildings grouped together must have been an exciting display of Chambers's architectural versatility.

Even more important for the future, however, was that Bute influenced Augusta to extend her late husband's garden of exotics to nine acres and that the remarkable William Aiton, who had been trained in the Chelsea Physick Garden, was engaged to manage them. He was in charge from 1760 until his death in 1793 and his green fingers induced many plants from very different climates and soils to flourish in those acres that became the embryonic 'Royal Botanic Gardens at Kew'.

Meanwhile, Augusta as Dowager Princess of Wales held court at the White House, with Lord Bute in a house nearby on Kew Green. By now he was playing many roles, including tutor to the future George III on constitutional history which shows Augusta's determination that her son should rule.

When the Prince came of age in 1756 at the age of 18 he moved from the White House to form his own household in the nearby Dutch House, so called because it had been built by a Dutch merchant in 1631, probably on the site of a house belonging to Queen Elizabeth's favourite, the Earl of Leicester. Once George moved in, the fairly modest Dutch House soon became known as Kew Palace, the name it bears today.

In 1760 George II died, as mentioned earlier, at Kensington Palace and the Prime Minister, the first Pitt, Earl of Chatham, drove down in his coach to pay his respects to the new King.

Of all the Hanoverians George III was 'The King of Kew'. It would have been understandable if he had reacted against the place where he had spent his youth under the tutelage of his formidable mother, but on the contrary when he became King he made Kew the centre of his life outside London. For forty years this was his haven from the troubles of the world as it has been for so many who have frequented the Gardens since.

Over the years the King made several major changes at Kew. Richmond Lodge was demolished and Queen Caroline's gardens turned into a farm which enabled George to pursue his highly professional agricultural interests. 'Capability' Brown was brought in to landscape the White House estate whilst Aiton was left to care for the botanic garden. To bring some diversity to what was a very flat piece of ground Brown got permission to use the battalion on guard duty to dig an artificial valley and planted laurels to give an atmosphere of mystery. Now this has become the Rhododendron Dell, one of the glories of Kew. Brown used all his magic to create a highly artificial 'natural' landscape with artfully contrived plantations and lawns transformed into meadows, the grass interspersed with the variegated colours of wild flowers.

One of George's ambitions when he was young had been to build a fine riverside palace for himself at Kew when he became King, and so when the time came Chambers was given the task of producing a design. It proved a long, and in the end, fruitless task for the architect. During the 1760s he produced plan after plan and in 1770 work was begun on one of them. The foundations were laid and the ground floor built, but then the King stopped further work. A last, more grandiose design which Chambers produced in 1775 finally came to nothing.

The likeliest reason was that when George's mother, Augusta, died in 1772 he took over the White House and moved there with his wife, Charlotte, and their steadily increasing family.

139

Charlotte had been 17 in 1761 when she married George, who was then 23. She bore him 15 children of whom only two died in childbirth.

For her George built at Kew 'The Queen's Cottage' as an 'away from it all' place for the family to play and have picnics. I have always thought it rather spooky and very Germanic in its setting of pine and fir trees.

These were the idyllic years for George and Charlotte at Kew. The boys lived in houses on the Green, but went up every morning to have breakfast with their parents, probably in Kew Palace, the old Dutch House. They then studied with their tutors or went to work on the adjacent farm: their father had earned by now the nickname, 'Farmer' George.

It was not, however, a closed society. On Thursdays the public was admitted to a large part of the Gardens, and could see the boys digging and hoeing or playing at single-wicket cricket. On Sundays the King and Queen with their family and entourage worshipped at St Anne's and would often walk along the tow-path towards Richmond, two by two, in seniority of age, whilst loyal subjects cheered them from their boats and bands played cheerfully from the decks.

It was, perhaps, a humdrum, homespun monarchy, but none the worse for that at a time when the glittering court of Versailles was about to be engulfed by revolution.

So far as the future of Kew was concerned, however, George's most significant act turned out to be the appointment of Sir Joseph Banks to take overall charge of the Botanic Gardens. A man of immense physical energy and insatiable intellectual curiosity, Banks had sailed with Captain Cook on his first journey to the South Seas and had shared with him the excitement of examining the vegetation of Australia around Botany Bay.

Banks realised that a world of undiscovered botanical specimens was opening up, especially for the British with their command of the seas. At Kew he worked without respite for nearly fifty years to obtain plants from every corner of the

Previous page: The Temperate House, one of the great masterpieces of Decimus Burton's genius.

Below: Queen Charlotte's Cottage, Kew. The State took over Kew Gardens in 1841, but Queen Charlotte's Cottage and its grounds remained a royal enclave until 1897 when Queen Victoria gave it to the nation to mark her Diamond Jubilee.

globe, often sending out enthusiastic young men on hazardous botanical missions from which they did not always return.

It was Banks who laid the foundations of Kew as an important botanic centre and his great successors in the 19th century, Sir William Jackson Hooker and his son, Sir Joseph Hooker, in turn enhanced its reputation and gave it world-wide renown. Men trained at Kew have since established its high standards in many lands. Kew is proud that its three-year Diploma is recognised throughout the world as a professional qualification of the highest standing. It was when the State took over the Gardens in 1841 that Kew was able to extend its work as a scientific institution. This is, indeed, still its primary function.

To return to George III, however, the sunlit years at Kew did not last. His attempt to carry out his mother's advice and rule (using a corrupt parliament) ended in disaster. Then the American colonies rose in revolt and, with the help of incompetent British generals and the French fleet, won their independence. To add to the King's troubles his sons, led by the Prince of Wales, showed signs of growing up dissolute and extravagant.

George had long suffered from nervous attacks, but in 1788 he became seriously ill mentally and was confined in the White House where he had spent so many happy years.* Fanny Burney, the novelist, who was a lady-in-waiting to the Queen, has related how on a walk she met the King with his attendants and fled in terror, pursued by George, who in the end did no more than give her a kiss. For those with a sympathetic nature the episode still casts a shadow over the peace and beauty of the Gardens George loved so well.†

He died in 1820 and the Prince Regent, who succeeded him as George IV, took no great interest in Kew. It was understandable for he had much else to occupy his considerable talents. There was the fabulous Royal Pavilion at Brighton, the building of Buckingham Palace, as well as the major development of Regent Street culminating in the creation of Regent's Park, and then finally the remarkable reconstruction of Windsor Castle. They were all considerable achievements in which he, as well as his architects, played a part.

On his death without issue in 1830, a younger brother, the Duke of Clarence, succeeded as William IV. He spent most of his time, when not in London on affairs of state, at Brighton or Windsor, but he had some affection for Kew where he had been

* The King had it pulled down in 1802.

† The King surprisingly recovered the next year, 1789, and remained in reasonably good health during the exhausting years of war with Revolutionary and Napleonic France. In 1811, however, when the tide of war was turning in Britain's favour, the King's madness returned, this time for good and the Prince of Wales was appointed Regent. George III spent his last nine, tragic years mainly at Windsor.

Following page: The Palm House, designed by Decimus Burton and Richard Turner, and built between 1844 and 1848.

Opposite: Bluebells near the Queen's Cottage.

Right: The lake at Kew Gardens.

increasingly a sad sight. Finally it had to be closed to the public, awaiting its fate. Fortunately, funds were finally provided for its grand reconstruction which began in 1977. The Queen performed the re-opening ceremony on Thursday 13th May 1982.

What a wonderful occasion! The celebrations included a reception, then later a concert and fireworks which momentarily brought light to the dark, sleeping groves of the Gardens.

That night, of all nights, should have given pleasure to so many shades of the Queen's family who over the centuries created Kew – a line of notable kings, queens, princes and princesses.

147

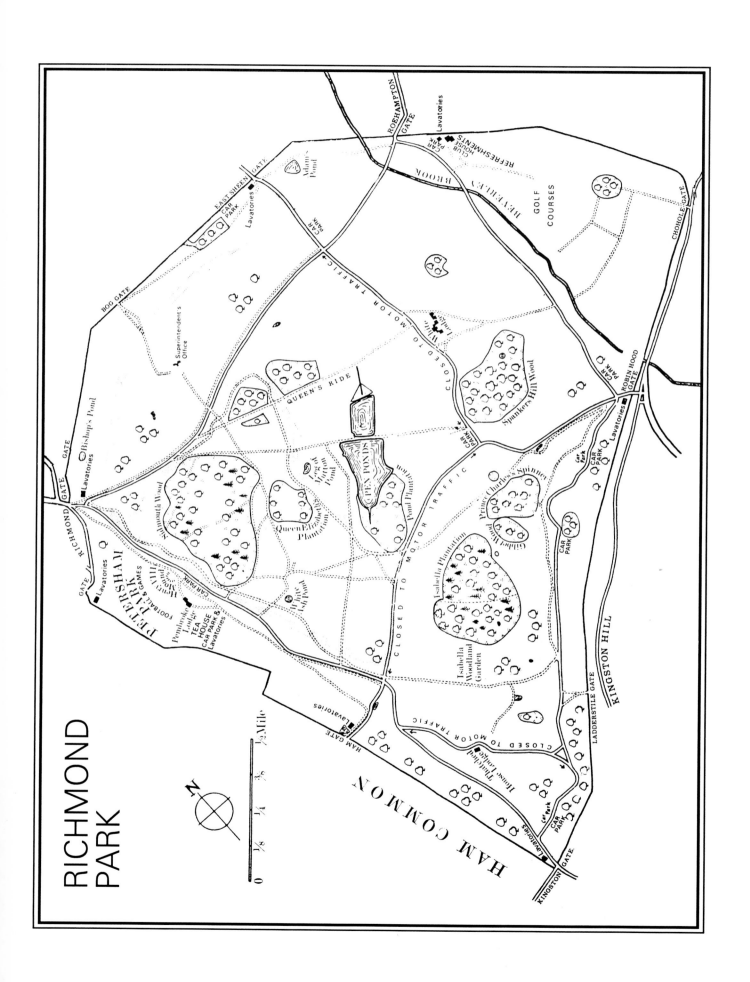

Richmond Park

THE LAND THAT lies along the Thames from Kew to Richmond and then rises up to the Park had been royal hunting grounds since the 13th century, and probably earlier. It was then called Sheen Chase, but when Henry VII, the first Tudor king, changed the name to his old earldom, Richmond, and built his riverside palace there, a closer connection began with the royal family which lasts to this day.

Alongside Pembroke Lodge by the road to Richmond gate is a hillock known as 'King Henry's Mount'. The popular tradition was – still is – that here Henry VIII stationed himself to wait for the rocket to rise from Tower Hill which would signal the beheading of his second wife, the formerly so passionately loved Anne Boleyn, mother of the future Queen Elizabeth. Now it has been proved, apparently, that the King was in Wiltshire on that day. Nevertheless, it seems most likely that the mound was an ancient burial ground, perhaps of some local king or prince, for its site commands a great stretch of the Thames valley.

Queen Elizabeth gave grand hunting parties at Richmond and they say her favourite, the Earl of Leicester, had a house by Kew Green. It was in Richmond Palace that the Queen died in 1603 after lying for days propped up by cushions on her low stool.

The Stuarts then came down from Scotland to inherit the throne through their descent from a sister of Henry VIII who had married a Scots king. The first of the line, King James I, left no great mark on Richmond, but his ill-fated son, Charles I, virtually created the Park. He was a great hunter and decided on one of his visits to Richmond Palace during an outbreak of plague in London that he would greatly extend the royal lands beyond the hill between Richmond and Kingston, buy out, if necessary compulsorily, any private owners and stock this 'New Park' not only with fallow deer, but with the larger red deer. The latter gave better sport, which meant they were more difficult to kill.

149

Amelia had blundered. The 'respectable persons' were members of the increasingly rich and influential middle class and they could strike back. They found a champion in John Lewis, a brewer of Richmond, who took legal action and finally obtained judgment in 1758 from an Assize Judge that the rights for pedestrians granted by Charles I must be respected. There was tremendous local jubilation. Lewis became a popular hero. When the ladder-stiles were replaced almost the entire population of the area climbed up and entered the Park. The news spread far and wide and reached the coffee-houses of London. It did the royal family no good.

Amelia fought on for a time, but gave up when her nephew, George III, came to the throne in 1760, and sold her Rangership to him for an annuity. She retired to Gunnersbury, across the river not far from her friend, Horace Walpole, the literary son of the Prime Minister, who lived in his famous 'little Gothic castle', Strawberry Hill, at Twickenham. The Princess died unmarried in 1786 at the age of 76.

Lord Bute, whose important role in the story of Kew Gardens we have recounted, now reappears. In 1761, a year after coming to the throne, George III appointed him Ranger of Richmond Park and he held the position until he died in 1792.

It seems likely that the King's mother, the widowed Princess Augusta, brought her considerable influence to bear for Bute was not only a close friend, but probably her lover and Richmond Park was only a few miles from Kew. It is worth noting that the relationship between Augusta and Bute lasted until her death in 1772, some proof that there was sincere affection, if not love, on both sides.

When Bute died the King took over as Ranger himself, made many improvements and had ambitions to create one of his model farms there, but his mental illness interrupted his plans. He did, however, greatly influence the future of the Park for he installed a friend, Henry Addington, later Lord Sidmouth and for a time Prime Minister, in White Lodge (as Stone Lodge was now named) and in 1813 appointed him Deputy Ranger. Sidmouth, who remained in the office until his death in 1844, largely shaped the Park that we know today.

The basic change was that the deer were no longer hunted, but farmed. The meat was and is distributed according to the Royal Venison Warrant which is a survivor from the Norman Forest Laws (for details see the Note on the Richmond Park Cull).

To add to the atmosphere of a farm, sheep and cattle were grazed and during the Napoleonic and Crimean Wars some of the land was put under plough (as it was in both World Wars in this century).

Sidmouth's lasting achievement, however, was the creation of protected plantations and coppices which as they developed fundamentally changed the appearance of the Park, turning it from open hunting ground to an estate planned partially for the preservation of game and partially for agreeable vistas.

Previous page: Pupils of The Royal Ballet School, White Lodge.

The largest of these plantations, Sidmouth Wood, recalls his work. Over the years I have appreciated the variety these coppices have given to the landscape, but they have always been gloomy enclaves, protected by railings not only against the depredation of the deer, but also against the public.

Obviously, this view was shared by some in authority for since the last war a woodland garden has been created in the Isabella Plantation which lies between Ham Gate and Robin Hood Gate. It is a beautiful garden, designed with such skill that nature, rather than man, seems to have formed the streams, the pools, the cascades and even the log bridges. Against a background of trees and tangled undergrowth paths meander leisurely among flowers of each season – bluebells, azaleas, magnolias, rhododendrons, camellias and heathers.

The garden is immensely popular and rightly so. No doubt part of its attraction is that a car park is situated nearby. It is useless to regret the days when people would have walked miles over the Park to find such a garden. This is the age of the motor-car.

Whilst Sidmouth was in the Park, the perennial struggle with the public flared up again. As Deputy Ranger he organised shooting parties, which often included royalty. There were now not only deer, but partridges, pheasants and hares, as well as plentiful rabbits. To keep the public away warnings were issued that wandering from the main paths could be dangerous.

The public – or, at any rate, the more unruly – responded by renewed poaching which included egg-stealing and mass clubbing of the red squirrels which had bred prolifically in the new plantations and coppices.

There were, however, more peaceful developments. An important adjoining estate of 59 acres, Petersham Park, was purchased in 1834 and added to the main Park. The elegant house was demolished as superfluous. Five years later Old Lodge, which had been the Walpoles' headquarters, was also pulled down. It was found to be beyond repair when it was being prepared as a residence for the new Ranger, the Duke of Cambridge, grandson of George III, and uncle of Queen Mary.

Queen Mary spent part of her early years in White Lodge which Queen Victoria kindly made available from time to time as an out-of-town residence to Mary's impecunious parents, Princess Mary Adelaide of Cambridge and the Duke of Teck.

It was at White Lodge in 1894 that Mary, now the wife of Prince George, later George V, gave birth to their first child, the ill-fated 'David' who having succeeded as Edward VIII in 1936, abdicated within a year to marry Mrs Simpson and spent the rest of his life in exile with her as the Duke of Windsor.

For White Lodge the 19th century was to prove the last grand royal epoch. It was, however, a very grand epoch indeed for Queen Victoria herself went to live there for a time to find solace in the Park after the death of her mother, the Duchess of Kent, in 1861.

The Duke of Cambridge, who was Ranger throughout the second half of the century, showed by his behaviour that the autocratic spirit of Princess Amelia lived on.

The Park was once more given over to the preservation of game and the deer for privileged shooting parties. Rights of access were restricted in yet another attempt to make the Park a private estate to which the public was only grudgingly admitted in certain areas on certain days.

It was King Edward VII who put an end to this attitude when he became Ranger in 1904. He gave orders that game should no longer be preserved in the Park and that as many of the woods as possible should be opened to the public. It proved to be the final act in the centuries-old struggle for the King was the last Ranger. Since then the Park has been administered like the other Royal Parks, by a government department, according to regulations laid down by Parliament.

White Lodge is now the home of the Royal Ballet School. Royalty, however, still lives in the Park for Princess Alexandra and her husband, Mr Angus Ogilvy, were granted Thatched House Lodge as a 'grace and favour' residence.

During the last war Richmond Park was rightly given over almost in entirety to the fight for survival. In the last forty years much has been done to restore those glorious two thousand acres and even to enhance their beauty. The heritage of Richmond Park has been safely passed on.

A Note on the Deer Cull

The Park is closed to the public between dusk and 7 a.m. in August and November every year, by order of the Secretary of State, Department of the Environment, which has responsibility for the Royal Parks. The restrictions on access are to protect the public from possible harm whilst a specified number of the deer are shot during the twice yearly cull.

Under the harsh Norman Forest Laws just about everything, living or dead, belonged to the Crown, including the great herds of deer that roamed over the country. Gradually, very gradually, permission to hunt the deer was granted, as a privilege. In addition, as a mark of royal favour, haunches of venison were presented to favoured subjects and corporate bodies. This was the origin of the Royal Venison Warrant, which still has to be signed by the Queen to authorise distribution of the cull in Richmond Park.

Following page: Light and shade in Richmond Park; Kingston Hill in the background.

157

Henry VIII, who succeeded his father in 1509, had been born at Greenwich. The rambling palace and the well-stocked park sloping to the river where sea-breezes gave a tang to the air were a treasured part of his youth. Not much more than 18 when he came to the throne, he was such a handsome, vigorous and intelligent Prince that he inspired enthusiasm and promised well for his country.

Inheriting great treasure amassed by a parsimonious father, Henry joyfully set about spending it – and Greenwich was one of the first to benefit from his open-handedness. Soon it well deserved its new name of Placentia, 'The Haunt of Pleasure'.

Henry was, indeed, a many-sided Renaissance Prince, as we have seen in St James's Park and Hampton Court. A tiltyard was, inevitably, a priority at Greenwich as elsewhere, so that he could exercise himself in the martial arts. Almost as important for him, however, were the carefully-railed flower gardens on which he spent a great fortune. Among them played fountains fed by intricate channels of water in the Italian style, and on the lawns strutted peacocks imported from abroad to add their jewelled beauty to the court. Unfortunately Henry's first Queen, Katherine of Aragon, found their harsh cries early in the morning broke her sleep and they were removed – perhaps to form part of one of those many-layered dishes that graced the royal banquets.

The most famous artists in Europe were attracted by Henry's munificence and his evident appreciation of their talents. The great German artist, Holbein, came over to work here for him and at Greenwich decorated two magnificent temporary halls erected in the tiltyard for the reception of the French Ambassador in 1527. Such receptions were not just formal welcoming parties, they were significant public relations exercises on which much time and money were lavished. The Tudors as a new dynasty realised they had to establish their credentials in a Europe suspicious of their stability.

Greenwich had formed Henry in his youth and now as King he exulted in his power to make changes which had long been near to his heart's desires. It was not all pleasure for he expanded the Royal Dockyards at nearby Woolwich and Deptford, thus laying the foundations of a modern efficient fleet. Such enterprises, though significant for the future, seem incidental, however, to the pattern of life Henry created at Greenwich with its joyous round of joustings, masques, revels, music, hunting, river parties, dalliance and love-making.

Apart from all these festivities Greenwich was very much Henry's family home. His three children who reigned after him were all born there – Mary, Elizabeth and Edward. Mary was the daughter of Katherine of Aragon whom he divorced to marry Anne Boleyn who bore him Elizabeth. Poor Jane Seymour, the third of his six wives, died there giving birth to

Opposite: The Queen's House, from Royal Observatory Hill, Greenwich.

179

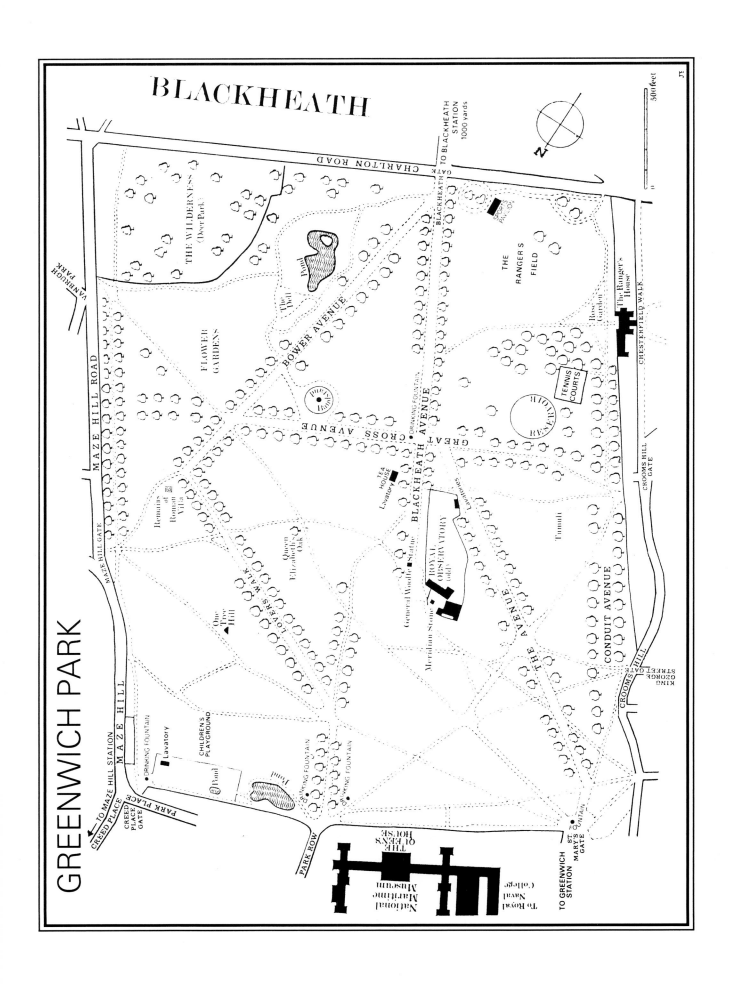

Edward the male heir Henry had so passionately desired for dynastic reasons.

The boy succeeded his father as Edward VI in 1547 at the age of ten and after a youth made miserable by ill-health and a rapacious Regency Council died six years later at Greenwich. He was followed by Mary who brought back Roman Catholicism, married Philip II of Spain and died at the age of 42, a sad, childless and almost friendless Queen.

Then in 1558 Elizabeth came to the throne, the last monarch of the Tudor dynasty and undoubtedly the greatest, for in her reign the country enjoyed considerable prosperity, spectacular victory over foreign foes and a miraculous flowering of poetry such as the world has rarely witnessed.

As well as those annual peregrinations round her kingdom, so ruinous to her hosts, Elizabeth liked to spend a few weeks at Greenwich each summer, at ease in the family atmosphere, walking in the gardens and the park beyond. She is said to have been partial to take refreshment in the hollow trunk of the great oak tree in whose shade her father, King Henry, had caressed her mother, Anne Boleyn.* The remains of the tree, 'Queen Elizabeth's Oak', which died only a hundred years ago, is still there behind railings not far from 'Lover's Walk'.

It was at Greenwich that Sir Walter Raleigh, the one paladin of Renaissance England, is reputed to have thrown down his costly cloak in the mud to smooth Elizabeth's path. Apocryphal or not, the story sheds light on the atmosphere of Gloriana's court where a gesture could make or, just as easily, break a man's career. A glittering, dangerous court, but then Machiavelli was her bedside reading!

When Elizabeth died in 1603, the Stuart King James, son of Mary, Queen of Scots whom she had beheaded in 1587, succeeded through Margaret Tudor, a sister of Henry VIII who had married James IV of Scotland.

James I was, we are told, 'the wisest fool in Christendom'. He certainly was a drunkard and a notorious pederast. His association with the handsome page, Robert Carr, later Earl of Somerset, led, however, to the enrichment of Greenwich with one of the most beautiful and influential buildings in England – the Queen's House.

King James's Queen was Anne of Denmark and as a woman of spirit she refused to attend the marriage of Carr to Lady Essex, a divorced woman of unsavoury reputation who was later found to be in addition a poisoner. The Queen had grown to like Greenwich during the court's summer visits there and James, knowing this, in desperation offered her the palace and grounds as the price of gracing the wretched nuptials.

Anne accepted the terms and in 1616 commissioned a

---

* The King later signed her death-warrant at Greenwich.

London architect, Inigo Jones, whose work her brother, Christian IV of Denmark, knew and admired, to build her a house at Greenwich between the old Tudor palace and the Park.

Inigo Jones, of humble birth, had been lucky as a youth to find a discerning patron in William Herbert, 3rd Earl of Pembroke, who financed his studies in Europe, especially in Italy where Palladio of Vicenza was at the time recreating classical architecture in a contemporary idiom.

On his return to England Inigo Jones gained royal favour, first with scenery for masques and festivities, but with the Queen's House at Greenwich he virtually founded the Renaissance style of English architecture. It was a revolution still with us, which has changed our environment, and his genius deserves a grander epithet that that of 'the English Palladio'.★

Anne of Denmark died in 1619 and work stopped on her house at Greenwich for nearly ten years. Then her son by James, Charles I, had it completed for his French Queen, Henrietta Maria. She returned to France as an exile following the Royalist defeat in the Civil War, but came back to England when her son, Charles II, was restored to the throne in 1660. At Greenwich she had the Queen's House enlarged somewhat, but fortunately the architect was John Webb, a pupil of Inigo Jones, so that the original proportions were respected.

We have seen how Charles II re-created St James's Park in the French style and left his patte d'oie mark on Hampton Court, but at Greenwich his plans were more ambitious. He demolished the old riverside Tudor palace, which had fallen into decay during the Commonwealth years, and decided to build a grand new palace which would vie with those of the French King.

John Webb designed for him a three-winged building round a courtyard facing the river. Work began in 1664 and one section, 'The King's House', was completed by 1669 when, as often happened with Charles II, money ran out. At the same time, however, the King had reshaped the Park in accordance with a design sent to him by André Le Nôtre, the great gardener of Louis XIV at Versailles and elsewhere.

It seems, however, that the classical French patte d'oie design of the period did not suit, or could not be implemented

★ The Banqueting House in Whitehall is the most widely known of Jones's work. It was built for James I between 1619 and 1622. Later, his son, Charles I, commissioned the Flemish master, Rubens, to paint a magnificent ceiling depicting the apotheosis of his father. The work earned the artist a large fee and a knighthood, both well-deserved. It is a tragic irony that Charles I stepped from that Banqueting House for his execution in 1649.

The design of the White House in Washington, DC, is sometimes said to have been influenced by the Queen's House. Certainly the official Presidential home does bear some resemblance, but on consideration this seems due to the fact that Jones's Palladian style had become by then an integral part of the architectural tradition for the design of residences of grace and dignity.

184

Previous pages: The Old Royal Observatory, designed by Christopher Wren for Charles II.

in the Park. The grand tree-lined Blackheath Avenue certainly stretches straight down from the top of the Park to the slope towards the river, but the intersecting avenues, The Avenue, Great Cross Avenue and the Bower Avenue do not fit, so far as one can tell, any overall plan. Perhaps the steep slope wrecked the Le Nôtre design, or perhaps money ran out again.

Palace or not, Le Nôtre gardens or not, Charles II left an indelible mark on Greenwich by commissioning Christopher Wren in 1675 to design an observatory in the Park for the Reverend John Flamsteed, the first Astronomer Royal, 'in order to the finding out of the longitude of places and for perfecting navigation and astronomy. . . .'

Thus was born the world-famous Royal Greenwich Observatory, Britain's first scientific institution and a lasting proof of the high intelligence behind the smiling mask of 'The Merry Monarch'. In 1948 the astronomers took themselves to Herstmonceux Castle in Sussex to set up their radio telescopes and computers in more spacious surroundings, but Flamsteed House remains at Greenwich. It is a splendid memorial, now open to the public, with the famous meridian line for Longitude 0, the bars of metal showing standard units of length, the beautiful Octagon Room with its superb Tompion clocks and in other rooms displays showing the development of chronometers and telescopes. The house, a remarkable structure of brick and stone, is built on the hill where Duke Humphrey had his watch-tower, so combining his literary scholarship with the scientific skills of poor Flamsteed, so meagrely and irregularly paid.

The Royal Hospital and Park at Greenwich, 1711.

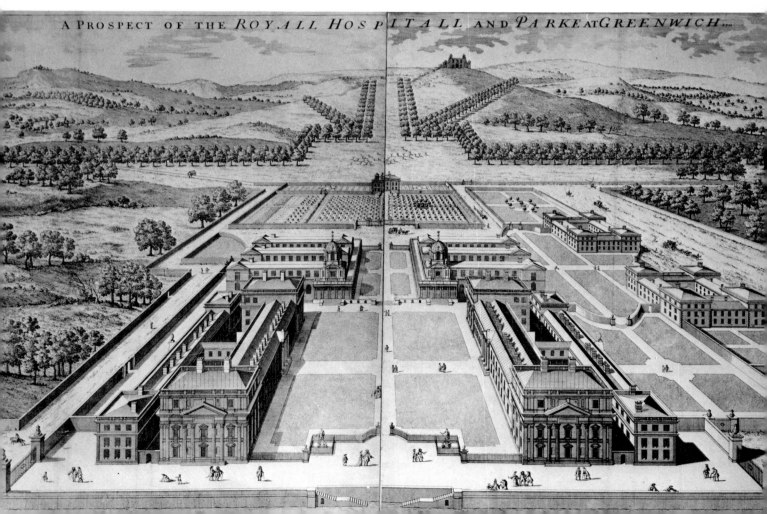

A PROSPECT OF THE ROYALL HOSPITALL AND PARKE AT GREENWICH

If you happen to be there at the right time it is fascinating to watch the red time-ball on the tower falling on its staff at exactly 1 p.m. It is from such precise techniques that man has since developed the knowledge to conquer space and make the H-Bomb!

Charles II died in 1685 and was succeeded by his brother, James II, who after three disastrous years fled the country in 1688 with his wife, Mary of Modena, who had recently given birth, (disputed by enemies), to a son, James 'the Old Pretender'. Mary of Modena had earlier been given the use of the Queen's House at Greenwich by her husband and it turned out that she was to be the last direct royal tenant.

William and Mary, who reigned jointly after 1688, made their home in Kensington and Hampton Court as we have seen, but they were responsible for those magnificent buildings that face the river at Greenwich on the site of the old palace, constituting one of the architectural glories of the English heritage.

Queen Mary, daughter of James II by Anne Hyde, had taken on the noble task of caring for the thousands of wounded seamen who came back after the costly victory of La Hogue over the French in 1692. She saw they were housed in the newly-built palace wing at Greenwich, but then conceived the idea of building a splendid home for ex-seamen there, which would complement the Royal Hospital at Chelsea built by her uncle, Charles II, for old soldiers. She knew William would rise to the ambitious plan to make Greenwich Hospital even grander than Les Invalides, built by the arch-enemy, Louis XIV, for his disabled veterans.

Wren was called in and produced a splendid design which, however, blocked out the view of the Queen's House. He was sent back to his drawing-board. Then, as we have earlier related, Mary died at Kensington from smallpox at the age of 32 in 1694. William was quite broken by his loss and reproached himself for not having pushed forward her plans at Greenwich. Wren provided a new design which left open the river view of the Queen's House by dividing the hospital into east and west wings. Each was surmounted by a noble dome, one above the chapel, the other above the Painted Hall, decorated by Sir James Thornhill and his assistants over twenty years (1707–27).

What a wealth of talent was available at that time to work at Greenwich! There was not only Wren, but Nicholas Hawksmoor and, later, Sir John Vanbrugh, who built himself a mock medieval castle to live in which still stands near the Maze Hill Gate of the Park.

It all took time and money, but the great project was finally completed by the middle of the 18th century. Well, perhaps not quite complete; for William had hoped to erect a statue of Mary in the main court that faces the river. But, as Macaulay, the classic historian of William's reign, writes:

'That part of the plan was never carried into effect; and few of those who now pass up and down the imperial river and gaze on the noblest of European hospitals are aware that it is a memorial of the virtues of the good Queen Mary, of the love and sorrow of William, and of the great victory of La Hogue.'

Greenwich became a worthy home for the sailors who survived the bloody battles and the harsh conditions of life below deck during those years when the Royal Navy under leaders such as Nelson won supremacy at sea and Britain found, almost to its surprise, that the world was for the taking at the end of the Napoleonic Wars in 1815. Over the years, more than 20,000 Pensioners died in peace at Greenwich and are remembered by a single, dignified memorial.

There was not a foreign fleet able to challenge Britain until the end of the 19th century when our old allies, the Germans, started to build, so that the number of Greenwich Pensioners had dwindled considerably by the 1860s. Some inmates had long complained that their surroundings were too grand for them and the discipline too rigid. The Board of Admiralty gradually found it convenient to give allowances to Pensioners to live with their families and in 1869 those remaining were removed to more modest quarters. For four years the hospital remained closed and then reopened with a flourish as the Royal Naval College, which has since rightly come to be known as the University of the Navy, where both Prince Philip and Prince Charles have been proud to study for their promotion examinations.

The great Painted Hall, which some, perhaps over-partial, believe to rival the Sistine Chapel in splendour, is now the officer's mess.

The change was probably inevitable and sensible. The buildings are now occupied by the men who will command the nuclear submarines, aircraft carriers (if any) and frigates of the future.

I sometimes wonder, however, what William and Mary would have thought about it all. They might smile at our claim to be more democratic now when their home for seamen has been turned into an élite college.*

As a mark of national gratitude to the Royal Navy a naval orphanage was established during the Napoleonic Wars in the Queen's House. New east and west wings were built in the attractive Regency style of the day and linked to the Queen's House, where the administrators and teachers lived, by the graceful colonnades you can use today.

* Chelsea Hospital, also designed by Wren, still fortunately retains its original function. The Great Hall has been restored since the war as the dining-room for the Pensioners.

London from Greenwich Park.

This 'Naval Asylum', to use the original name, together with the older Royal Hospital School with which it was amalgamated, cared for and educated as many as 900 boys at a time. By 1924 the buildings were no longer appropriate and a benefactor gave the money for a new school at Holbrook on the River Stour in Suffolk which was opened in 1933.

Now the Queen's House and its outstretched wings was ready for a metamorphosis into the National Maritime Museum. In one lifetime this has earned an enviable international reputation, thanks to splendid gifts and bequests and the inspired leadership of Frank Carr, who was Director from 1947–60, the crucial formative years.

It is a treasure-house for scholar and student and an absorbing attraction for any visitor with its 900 ships' models, its collection of 3,600 oil paintings and 30,000 prints and drawings. It is always hard to leave the galleries, so fascinating are they.

By Greenwich Pier near by you cannot miss the tall masts, spars and intricate rigging of the *Cutty Sark* (963 tons gross), one of the great tea-and-wool clippers, launched on the Clyde in 1869, now preserved as a tribute to the ships and men of the Merchant Navy. After a somewhat chequered history in this century she was after the last war finally accepted as a gift by a special Cutty Sark Society of which the Duke of Edinburgh was the driving force. The LCC (later the GLC) generously provided the site and built the dock. On 25 June 1957 the Queen came down to Greenwich and declared the ship open to the public.

The venture has proved a quite remarkable success. Millions have queued to visit the ship. The initial debt was quickly paid off by admission charges. Winter evening classes in seamanship and navigation run by the GLC often have waiting-lists.

To complete this saga of the sea Sir Francis Chichester's *Gypsy Moth IV* has also found a lasting berth at Greenwich not far from the *Cutty Sark*, which overwhelmingly dwarfs her. That is not inappropriate for it exemplifies the remarkable qualities of seamanship and courage shown by Francis Chichester (1902–72). In 1966 he sailed his small craft into Sydney harbour after a 107-day single-handed voyage from Plymouth, and then back again round the Horn. He richly deserved the accolade of knighthood given him by the Queen and his example has since been followed by others, younger, but scarcely more daring.

Greenwich Park itself had a poor time in the 18th and early 19th centuries; in the first decades of the 18th the hospital was being built and much of the area was not much more than a busy builder's yard. There was a day of glory in 1714 when George, the Elector of Hanover, landed at the pier with his German court, including his mistresses, Mesdames Kielmansegge and Schulenberg. Here he was humbly greeted as King George I by the secretly sneering Establishment – archbishops, bishops, noble peers, among them John Churchill, the Duke of Marlborough, the great soldier, the great betrayer.

The Hanoverians, however, never showed any great interest in Greenwich, preferring, as we have seen, Kensington Gardens, Kew and Hampton Court. It is understandable, for the new seamen's hospital effectively finished Greenwich as a home and Park for royalty.

The area surrounding the Park, however, still had residential prestige and several fine mansions were built, especially on the west side, some of which still stand.

Macartney House for example, was bought by General Edward Wolfe in 1751. His famous son, James Wolfe, stayed there between campaigns and it was from Greenwich that he left for America. He won immortal fame and death at the age of 32 on 13th September 1759, when he successfully stormed the Heights of Abraham before Quebec and in one day won Canada for Britain from the French.

It was not until shortly before World War II that a statue was raised to General Wolfe here, but the site chosen is magnificent. It stands dramatically at the apex of the tree-lined Blackheath Avenue and looks down the steep slope to the incomparable view beyond of the Queen's House, the Royal Naval College and the river.

The naval connection is appropriate for Wolfe's victory was made possible by the presence of the Royal Navy. It was an example of what has become known as 'a combined operation'.

The statue was unveiled by a direct descendant of the Marquis de Montcalm, the brilliant strategist and administrator, who fell aged 47 in the same battle as Wolfe. Montcalm's far-seeing plan had been to pin down the British colonies to the coast of North America by a series of forts to the west. J. R. Green in his *History of the English People* writes that the elimination of the French removed the one enemy the colonists feared, opened up the boundless plains of the West and laid the foundations of the United States.

So the statue of General Wolfe is a worthy place of pilgrimage for the many Americans who visit Greenwich. They and ourselves, for that matter, might reflect that like so many of the English leaders who achieved greatness he was an unconventional, difficult, temperamental man, subject to terrible fits of depression. So much for the myth of the strong, silent Empire builder!

The Ranger's House, a little to the south of Macartney House, was in the 18th century Chesterfield House, a semi-country home of Philip Stanhope, 4th Earl of Chesterfield. He was a 'grand seigneur' of considerable standing who is remembered, not often favourably, for his 'Letters to his Son', who was another Philip Stanhope, his natural son by a French-woman. Dr Johnson's crushing dictum that the letters inculcated 'the manners of a dancing master and the morals of a whore' has won wide acceptance. I find the judgment harsh for my copy of the Letters has long given me pleasure as a window into an elegant 18th-century world, dominated by French culture, then at a peak of achievement.

It was a cynical, self-seeking world, but when has it not been? Chesterfield is adept at concealing the brutal ugliness of life with a sheen of artificial grace.

From Greenwich he wrote to his son, then in Paris, on 6th June (OS) 1751:

'I should have thought that Lord ————, at his age, with his parts and address, need not have been reduced to keep an opera whore in such a place as Paris, where so many women of fashion generously serve as volunteers. I am still more sorry that he is in love with her. . . .'

In the early 19th century Chesterfield House became the grace and favour residence of the Ranger of the Park, an office of dignified ease, made easier with a handsome income. Arthur, Duke of Connaught, held the post for a time in his long life (1850–1942). The reforming Victorian Field-Marshal, Lord Wolseley, who took over Egypt for Britain, was also Ranger of the Park during his later years.

The house was acquired in 1902 by the LCC (later the GLC), suffered severe bomb damage during the last war, but was restored with great care and expertise. It has since become the

Previous page: 'Easter Monday in Greenwich Park' (from an engraving by Rawle, in the *European Magazine* of 1802).

home of the distinguished Suffolk Collection of 16th and early 17th-century paintings of royalty and their courts. The GLC proved a gracious patron of the arts, making the Grand Salon in the south wing available for occasional concerts of chamber music, art exhibitions and meetings.

Stretching beyond the house is the large 'Ranger's Field' which runs as far as Blackheath Avenue. First there is a very fine rose-garden whose beds are in their season a delight to the eye and nose. The rest of the field is given over to sport with tennis courts and pitches for cricket, rugby and hockey.

The Prince Regent, so active elsewhere as we have related, played only a negative rôle at Greenwich. His estranged wife, the unfortunate Caroline of Brunswick, lived in a large mansion, Montague House, by Chesterfield Gate with the sinecure post of Ranger. It was here she was alleged to have been 'highly indiscreet', an accusation somewhat ludicrous from her promiscuous husband. When she finally left the country in 1815 the Prince Regent in his fury had Montagu House demolished and all that remains is 'Queen Caroline's Sunken Bath', a pathetic pit about four feet by five and six feet deep.

Across Blackheath Avenue is an enchanting area, where you can walk under great trees to a delightful flower garden and a romantic lake where wild-fowl swim among the weeping willows. Beyond is the Wilderness, where behind a protective wire fence, a small herd of fallow deer and a few red deer browse in peace. By their presence they continue a tradition that goes back to the first enclosure of this ancient park.

With a bandstand where music is regularly played in the summer months, an equally popular tea pavilion, a large children's playground and boating pond, even a few Roman ruins and graves, Greenwich Park has a world of interest to offer. Some of the people who stroll there come from the surrounding areas; many more are visiting what has become over the years a noble tribute to the maritime history of an island race. It is also, thanks to a devoted Superintendent and staff, a very beautiful Park.

When I was a boy I used to be taken to Greenwich by river from St Katherine's Docks by the Tower of London. Beyond Tower Bridge it was a slow journey among a forest of masts of the fleets of ships from all over the world which used the great Port of London. It gave me, perhaps foolishly, a sense of pride and after the war I felt even greater pride when I heard of the heroism of those who lived, often in poverty, in Dockland. In spite of very heavy and consistent bombing they had kept the Port open and the spirit of defiance alive.

Just over ten years ago we were going by launch to Greenwich from the Tower as usual and soon the truth was forced on me that Dockland was not just derelict, but dead. For years I had been reading about the decay of the Port and the rise of the great

new containerisation ports at Tilbury and Felixstowe, but the actual scene of desolation I witnessed that day was a revelation that silenced me.

Now most of those great docks, built mainly in the 19th century, have been demolished, but a new life is, somewhat slowly, burgeoning. The air is cleaner, thanks to the anti-pollution laws passed by the Wilson Labour administrations in the sixties, so that the buildings of our heritage, once cleaned, are again revealed – as they were, more or less. As I was completing this account I came across a newspaper advertisement for fashionable luxury flats which have just been built on the river bank opposite Greenwich.

With the Queen's House, Inigo Jones virtually founded the Renaissance style of English Architecture. The Queen in question was King James I's wife, Anne of Denmark.

194

train of artillery bombarded the castle walls for seven hours, but the garrison held out and in time Cromwell's New Model Army exercised in the Home Park and beyond while Royalist officers, taken prisoner during the war, watched helplessly from the terraces.

Previous page: Windsor Castle, from the Long Walk.

In 1648 Cromwell and his captains held a solemn three-day prayer meeting in St George's Chapel (begun by Edward IV in 1475 and completed by Henry VII and VIII) where the Knights of the Garter had for many years had their stalls. The Parliamentarian leaders were in no mood of courtly chivalry for they solemnly vowed to put an end to 'the man of blood', Charles Stuart. He was executed the following year in Whitehall (30th January 1649) and his headless body was brought to Windsor a few days later and buried under the floor of St George's Chapel.

To return to the Great Park, it is appropriate to start at the castle from the George IV Gateway which the Prince Regent created when he became King. This was part of his plan to transform Charles II's Long Walk into a royal avenue leading to Snow Hill and the massive equestrian statue by Westmacott of his father, George III, now called 'The Copper Horse'.

A strange man indeed, George IV, to pay such a noble tribute to a father with whom, in the Hanoverian tradition, he was almost always on such bad terms. For the King commemorated, the statue has a pathetic side. There he is set grandly in the centre of parkland where he lived rather simply, looking after his farms, walking with his wife Charlotte and their growing brood of children, warmly acknowledging loyal greetings and chatting to young visitors. Those happy years were followed by the agony of mental derangement when the poor old King was detained at Windsor, watched by attendants as he wandered through the Park, half-blind and from time to time stopping to talk to trees he thought were people.

It was George III who had begun the Gothic restoration of the castle, using the talents of James Wyatt. By the time George IV came to the throne the Gothic revival had triumphed. It is ironic that the King, who with his architect Nash had done so much earlier for classical architecture, now presided over the comprehensive restructuring of Windsor Castle which made it a masterpiece of Picturesque Gothic and by far the most prestigious royal palace in the kingdom. James Wyatt's nephew, Jeffry, won the commission and completed the work. Some experts consider him to have been less than first-class, but the work brought him fame, a knighthood and permission to change his name so that he ended as Sir Jeffry Wyatville.

The elm trees with which Charles II lined the Long Walk had to be cut down in 1945, but the replacements are now sturdy young trees, similar perhaps to those George IV would have seen when he drove himself through the Park in a light two-horse open carriage. He could well have had young Victoria, the

200

future Queen, as passenger, and he would doubtless have shown her his menagerie which included birds of exotic plumage, kangaroos from Australia and a giraffe given him by Mehemet Ali, Pasha of Egypt.

Overweight and drowsy with too much food and alcohol though he was, the King enjoyed his pleasures at Windsor. There was – and is still – the two-mile drive known as Rhododendron Walk which he planted between Bishops Gate and Virginia Water and which flowers magnificently in May and June.

There were other pastimes. Perhaps he might feel like fishing in Virginia Water from the verandah of his Chinese fishing pavilion, elaborately decorated with fearsome gilded dragons. Or perhaps he might command an alfresco banquet in the Roman ruins of Leptis Magna which had been brought for him from Libya. A few friends, perhaps his mistress, Lady Conyngham, would join him while a small group of musicians played from a barge on Virginia Water. It was a very agreeable, sybaritic way to pass his remaining years.

Since that time the extensive Valley Gardens have been created on the northern banks of Virginia Water.

Not far away are the Savill Gardens, superbly landscaped, which were made out of a tangled wilderness by George VI's friend and gardening adviser after whom they are named. The King did not have an easy life and found great solace in planning and realising the Gardens with Savill. They are a memorial to a King who showed courage and endurance all his life.

Smith's Lawn has enjoyed public fame since the war as a polo ground, for first Prince Philip and then Prince Charles played there and many members of the royal family, including the Queen, came to watch. Press and public followed.

For the Queen, Windsor is the favoured home, with Balmoral as the beloved Highland retreat in late summer and early autumn. To call Windsor 'a home' is slightly absurd for it is a great palace and castle rolled into one vast complex. The private apartments that lie behind the South and East Terraces of the Upper Ward are very extensive indeed and do not take into account the magnificent suite of State apartments which may be visited when the Queen is not in residence.

There are superb private gardens beyond the East Terrace and outside the castle are extensive stables. All in all, Windsor, with an almost incomparable art collection which includes the Leonardo drawings, and its fine furniture and tapestries is outstanding among royal residences.

As young girls, the Queen and her sister, Princess Margaret, spent the war years there guarded by a specially trained group of Guards officers who, with hindsight, were doing a more important job than might have been thought, for towards the end of the war Hitler's daring SS commandos were quite capable of dropping out of the skies and taking hostages.

Following pages: The Long Walk, Windsor (left), and Savill Gardens (right).

201

Perhaps it was those war years that wove a protective cocoon round the Queen to which she is always trying to return. During the months in London at Buckingham Palace she is off to Windsor after lunch on Friday and not back until mid-morning Monday – unless there are essential duties.

Christmas used traditionally to be spent at Sandringham, but the Queen now gathers the whole royal family round her at Windsor to celebrate what she considers the great family festival of the year in the family home.

For the Queen, Ascot Week in June is the other great occasion based on Windsor. It is the Royal meeting, founded at nearby Ascot by that redoubtable huntress, Queen Anne, in the early 18th century. As a lifelong owner and breeder of racehorses, the present Queen looks forward to the meeting every year, but it is not only for the racing; it is a great social event when the Queen entertains royally at Windsor Castle.

Whether she is riding in the Park, perhaps with a notable guest such as President Reagan, or walking in the gardens with her family, the castle dominates the scene.

Yet when you look at the famous skyline if you are out walking in Windsor Great Park, the building does not frown on the surrounding countryside as a castle is traditionally supposed to do. You could say it wears a smile – dignified, of course!

The Parks Superintendent

SINCE THE AUTUMN of 1983 Mrs Jennifer Adams has occupied the highly-coveted post of Superintendent of the four central Royal Parks in London – St James's, The Green Park, Hyde Park and Kensington Gardens. She is also responsible for a number of other less public, but important gardens such as the Queen's 43 acres behind Buckingham Palace and the smaller patch behind the Prime Minister's official residence at No 10 Downing Street.

She lives near Hyde Park with her husband in a graceful early Victorian 'tied' house. The rent is 10% of her salary of £14,000 p.a.

Her appointment came as a bombshell to a traditionally-minded male hierarchy. There were many who were against the choice of a woman. There were others who considered she lacked the width of experience necessary for the job. I think she has the strength of character to combat the doubters. In the medium run, however, all depends on her performance.

She is a Londoner who in her teens became so interested in botany that she determined to train as a gardener. In 1964, a time of opportunity for British youth, she was accepted at the age of 16 as an indentured apprentice by the Royal Parks and served her six years, mainly in Regent's Park, working for the customary pittance. She not only saw it through all the stages from washing flower-pots, she earned a place for a year's training at the Institute of Parks and Recreation College at Pangbourne in Berkshire. She came out with the Diploma of Parks and Recreation Management, having given her dissertation on 'Recreation in an Urban Environment'.

Then Wandsworth Borough Council gave her a managerial post dealing with maintenance, horticulture and landscaping, and in 1974 at the age of 26 she was appointed Parks Superintendent in charge of a staff of 400 and a generous budget. After nine years in Wandsworth she decided on a change of scene. The Central Parks post became vacant and was advertised. She applied – and got it.

She told me that she had been well aware the post would involve her in 'politics'. She did not mean 'party politics'. It was just a sensible realisation that her responsibilities would by their very nature make her subject to pressure from many influential quarters and that she would need the skills of a diplomat to survive.

Park superintendents and managers up and down the country have their problems keeping councillors and the public reasonably happy, but the Superintendent of the central Parks has to walk a path through a minefield of dangerous situations almost daily.

So far as the gardens of Buckingham Palace are concerned there is a staff of eight gardeners with their own superintendent, Mr Fred Kemp, who has been there 37 years, but Mrs Adams is ultimately responsible.

She also has in her care the Queen Mother's garden at Clarence House, and the gardens at St James's Palace and Kensington Palace where other members of the royal family have their London homes.

In Downing Street the gardens of No 10 and No 11 (the official residence of the Chancellor of the Exchequer) are communal and this has given Mrs Thatcher the opportunity to make many changes in the whole area. She has had new flower-beds planted, with the emphasis on roses. The lawns and gravel paths have to be maintained to the highest standards. No 10 is notable for its lavish floral decorations, drawing on the resources of the extensive Royal Parks nurseries in Hyde Park.

The full list of Mrs Adams's responsibilities is awesome, even if, as she told me, the work involved may be in some cases only slight. Here are some of the locations:

Parliament Square; the Houses of Parliament; Admiralty House; Lancaster House; Marlborough House; Trafalgar Square; the National Gallery; the Tate Gallery; the Victoria and Albert Museum and Grosvenor Square.

Comments on the gardens may come from the Queen herself or some other member of the royal family, government ministers, members of Parliament, senior civil servants and so on and so on. All these are people who can make their views known and expect action to be taken.

Before the cuts started to be made a few years ago the Central Parks were run with a staff of 250. When I met Mrs Adams in 1984 numbers had been reduced to 176, a reduction of 30 per cent. She told me that there were whispers that the recruitment freeze might thaw a little later in the year.

Like most other managers staff problems take up a lot of her time, but she is luckier than most for the Civil Service tries hard to look after its own and, in addition, the Royal Parks have an enviable reputation of attracting men and women who are dedicated to their work.

Acknowledgements

Whilst accepting responsibility for the selection of illustrations, the Publishers wish to express their grateful thanks for the advice and guidance received from Mr Peter Knight and from the Tasiemka Archives.

The line illustrations are the result of extensive research on the part of Mr Peter Knight, who also commissioned the original photographs taken by Count Fritz von der Schulenburg.

The Publishers also gratefully acknowledge the following sources of illustrations:
  The Property Services Agency of the Department of the Environment.
  The Royal Institute of British Architects.
  The Illustrated London News.
  The Graphic.
  Illustrated Times.
  Harper's New Monthly Magazine.